GO
BACK
and Be HAPPY

GO
BACK
and Be HAPPY

Reclaiming Life After a Devastating Loss

Julie Papievis

as told to Margaret McSweeney

MONARCH
BOOKS

Oxford, UK & Grand Rapids, Michigan, USA

Published in association with the Books & Such Literary Agency, Janet Kobobel Grant, 52 Mission Circle, Suite 122, PMB 170, Santa Rosa, CA 95409-5370, www.booksandsuch.biz.

First published in the UK in 2008 by Monarch Books
(a publishing imprint of Lion Hudson plc),
Wilkinson House, Jordan Hill Road, Oxford OX2 8DR.
Tel: +44 (0)1865 302750 Fax: +44 (0)1865 302757
Email: monarch@lionhudson.com
www.lionhudson.com

ISBN: 978-1-85424-871-8 (UK)
ISBN: 978-0-8254-6276-4 (USA)

Distributed by:
UK: Marston Book Services Ltd, PO Box 269,
Abingdon, Oxon OX14 4YN;
USA: Kregel Publications, PO Box 2607,
Grand Rapids, Michigan 49501

This book has been printed on paper and board independently certified as having come from sustainable forests.

British Library Cataloguing Data
A catalogue record for this book is available from the British Library.

Printed and bound in Wales by Creative Print & Design.

ACKNOWLEDGEMENTS

A friend recently sent this message to me in an e-mail: 'Friends are angels who lift us to our feet when our wings have trouble remembering how to fly.'

I would like to thank those special people who never allowed me to give up on myself. Words cannot express how, each in your own way, you have helped me to accept and share the gift of grace that I have been given. First, and most importantly, my parents, Mary Ann and Jerry Papievis: I would not have recovered without their constant love and care. My sister Tammy Possidoni and her husband John and son Clayton. My brother Brett Papievis and his wife Lisa, and their sons Avery and Travis. My large extended family. My amazing 'medical dad' and neurosurgeon Dr John Shea, and Dr Neil Margolis, the person who helps me see. The paramedics, on duty and off, who responded to the scene. My employers and friends Tony Romanucci and Stephan Blandin. My counselor and confidante Sister Valerie Kulbacki. Loyola University Medical Center and Marianjoy Rehabilitation Hospital. The Rehabilitation Institute of Chicago and Midwest Brain Injury Clubhouse for the opportunity to participate in their Peer Support and Advocacy programs. ThinkFirst and Central DuPage Hospital for the opportunity to speak at local schools about injury prevention. The Spinal Cord Association and Brain Injury Association for their personal support throughout my recovery process and for their continued presence in my life. My best friends Jill Crosby and Sue Bentel, and their families. My triathlon coach Carol and my teammates Angie, Jina, and Laura. They encouraged me to go that extra mile. Milt Nelms, an international swim coach who graciously helped me to learn how to swim again. Bridget Tarrant, my physical therapist who taught me to run again. The people whom I call 'God's little elves,' my various counselors and therapists.

I would also like to thank these special people who made this book possible. My Aunt Kathy and Uncle Peter DiIorio, who have been constant pillars in my life; Susan and Rick Roman, who graciously helped me wrap this book with joy; my talented photographer Blair Holmes; Pam Montagno; my co-author and friend Margaret McSweeney, whose writing became the voice of my heart; my literary agent Janet Kobobel Grant, and Toni Rapach, a witness to my accident who is now a dear friend. A heartfelt thank you to the producers at Lifetime Television, ABC, WGN, CNN, TLN, *Chicago Sun Times*, *First for Women Magazine*, *Today's Chicago Woman*, and the staff at *Woman's Day Magazine* and *The Chicago Tribune* for first featuring my story.

And, of course, I wish to acknowledge and thank God for allowing me to 'go back and be happy.'

Humility

I asked God for strength,
that I might achieve –
I was made weak,
that I might learn humbly to obey.
I asked for help,
that I might do greater things –
I was given infirmity,
that I might do better things.
I asked for riches,
that I might be happy –
I was given poverty,
that I might be wise.
I asked for all things,
that I might enjoy life –
I was given life,
that I might enjoy all things.
I got nothing that I asked for –
but everything I had hoped for.
Despite myself,
my prayers were answered.
I am, among all men,
most richly blessed.

Unknown author

CONTENTS

FOREWORD

Julie Papievis is truly a miracle. During my thirty years as a neurosurgeon, I have never witnessed such a miraculous recovery as hers. On the evening that Julie was brought into Loyola University Medical Center's Trauma Unit in Maywood, Illinois, I was on call. Julie was completely unresponsive to light, sound, or touch. She had a severe brain stem injury, and her prognosis was grim.

For a doctor, one of the most difficult responsibilities is to tell a family that their loved one will either die, remain in a coma, or awaken without a functional life because of traumatic brain injuries. Someone once asked me if there is a cure for traumatic brain injuries. The answer is yes: prevention! Most traumatic brain injuries can be avoided if proper precautions are taken: drive safe, play safe, be safe.

With the severity of Julie's injuries, I did not even expect her to survive the night. I tried to prepare Julie's parents for the likelihood of her death. All that was left for anyone to do was to pray. In life's darkest moments, faith can shine like a beacon as prayer becomes a compass.

Still in a coma, Julie was transferred to a rehabilitation center. Months later, when she walked into my office, I was in complete shock. I honestly thought that she had died.

Over these past fifteen years, Julie has not ceased to amaze me. She overcame depression, ran in a 5K race only six years after her accident, participated in a triathlon and became a voice for the 'silent epidemic' of traumatic brain injury. Julie received a gift of recovery, and in return, she continues to give much of herself to others who face overwhelming circumstances. Her story offers hope to those without help, and she advocates for those who are disabled. I consider Julie to be not only a patient but also a lifelong friend who has made a difference in my life.

Dr John Shea, MD

Professor of Neurosurgery

Loyola University Medical Center

CHAPTER ONE

A WRECKED LIFE:
10 MAY 1993 AT 6:55 P.M.

Pulling her short brown hair, Toni Rapach screamed over the blaring song on the car radio, 'Honk your horn, TJ! Hurry! Honk your horn!'

The couple watched in disbelief as a large burgundy Oldsmobile Cutlass ran a red light and violently struck the driver's side of a small white Mazda sports car turning left out of a shopping mall in a Chicago suburb.

Toni jumped from her car and shouted, 'Somebody call 911!'

An older couple raced toward the accident scene. The wife shouted over to Toni, 'We're calling 911 right now on our cell phone, and my husband's a doctor!' In 1993, a mobile phone was not a common item.

Toni burst into tears when she looked into the Mazda and saw an unconscious young woman with a mane of blonde hair. She watched helplessly as the woman's head lay against the chest as if it was disconnected from her body. Toni turned around and shouted, 'Please, somebody help!' 'This poor girl and her family,' she sobbed, 'they will never be the same.'

The gathering crowd rushed to the crumpled car and tried to open the driver's door, which was streaked with burgundy paint from the Oldsmobile. The forceful impact had left both axles broken on the Mazda. A man ran to the other side of the car and managed to climb into the tangled debris. As he reached behind to pick up the young woman's head, the doctor instructed, 'Don't move her.'

'I'm an off-duty paramedic,' the man answered in a calm and confident manner. 'I know what I'm doing.'

'Go ahead then. I'm here if you need anything.'

The paramedic happened to be a block away from the accident scene, getting his tires fixed. He lifted the woman's head from her chest and cleared the airway so oxygen could pass to the brain. At 6:57 p.m., just two minutes after the accident, firefighters and paramedics arrived in a whir of sirens and flashing lights. Realizing the severity of the accident, Lieutenant Jim Streu radioed in a call to the station: 'Extrication equipment is needed at the scene. Send in the fire truck.'

Paramedics Greg Sauchuk and Randy Deicke leaped out of Ambulance 61. Racing to the scene with his first aid box, Greg said, 'Oh, man, this is really bad.'

They faced a 'Trauma Red' and time was a major concern. Two minutes of the 'Golden Hour' had already ticked away. Comprehensive medical treatment within that golden hour was imperative to offer any hope. Opening the first aid box, Greg removed some medical instruments to assess the woman's condition. He recognized his off-duty paramedic friend who was holding the woman's neck from the backseat of the car. Chips of sparkling glass surrounded the Mazda like Mardi Gras beads. Reaching through the blown out window, Greg said, 'Tom, how did you manage to even climb into this pretzel? Thanks for stabilizing her neck and clearing the airway.'

Greg checked the woman's breathing and said, 'Amazing. I feel a pulse. She doesn't need CPR.'

Lifting the woman's eyelids, Greg checked the pupils with a small flashlight. They didn't react. 'Pupils dilated and fixed,' Greg reported to Randy and then shouted, 'Hey, Miss! Can you hear me?'

The woman remained silent. With his large six-foot-three, 245-pound frame, Greg pressed his fist into the woman's chest. She didn't even flinch.

'Patient is unresponsive to pain with sternum rub,' Greg said. 'She scores a three.' Greg rated the woman on the Glasgow Coma Scale, a quick, practical and standardized system developed in 1975 for assessing the level of consciousness and predicting the ultimate outcome of a coma. A three was the lowest score out of a possible fifteen.

'I'll check her vitals,' Randy said as he wrapped the vinyl cuff around the woman's arm to check for blood pressure. He placed the stethoscope on the inner arm and pumped the rubber ball. No reading. He tried again. 'I can't even hear the blood flow,' Randy said, and shook his head while placing his fingertips on the woman's artery to check for a pulse. 'Patient's palpable blood pressure is only eighty. Not good. Looks like a traumatic brain injury. Probably brain stem. Elevated heart rate is 120. This is bad, guys. She's in shock. Possible internal damage. After this car door is off, let's do a "scoop and run".'

Within a minute, the fire truck arrived with the 'jaws of life' equipment. Al Green, another paramedic, was also on the truck along with firefighter Tony Pascolla. Tony lifted the forty-pound Hurst equipment and steadied the hydraulic spreader as he ripped the car door from its hinges. 'I'll be done in two minutes,' Tony shouted over the loud noise.

The paramedics decided against calling a helicopter since time was essential. Because of the severity of her injuries, they agreed to take the woman to a Level I Trauma Center instead of the nearest hospital. Loyola University Medical Center in Maywood, Illinois, was fourteen miles away. They knew that neurosurgeon Dr John Shea was her only hope. The ambulance left the scene at 7:12 p.m. and arrived at 7:25 p.m. Randy, Greg and Al pulled the stretcher out of the ambulance and ran into the emergency entrance to hand the woman over to the trauma team. 'She's posturing!' Randy said. They watched as the woman started extending her arms and legs in primitive reflexes, a sign that her body could not regulate itself. She then urinated all of the water from her body, soaking the stretcher, and started agonal breathing, the last breaths taken before dying.

As Greg walked back with Randy and Al toward the ambulance, he glanced over his shoulder at the lifeless body being carted away by the trauma team. 'Dear God,' he prayed, 'Please help her through this. Just help her through this.' He climbed into the driver's seat and left the hospital. He'd seen it before. He knew firsthand that traumatic brain injury is the number one killer of people forty-four years old and younger.

CHAPTER TWO

TURNING LEFT: A CHANGE IN LIFE'S DIRECTION

My inbox looked like Mount Everest, with phone calls to return and paperwork to complete – reminders of my responsibilities as a benefits administrator and accounts receivable manager. After working ten hours, I still felt far behind on my first day back from vacation. The white beaches of Cancun were mirages in my drab office surrounded by white concrete walls. My Mexican vacation was a great getaway – a temporary escape from my feelings of uncertainty after my divorce and a welcome change from my intensive training for an upcoming biathlon race.

I leaned back in my desk chair for a quick break. I had made it through a whole year of being on my own. That was a big accomplishment. When my marriage failed as a result of deep and personal irreconcilable differences, I felt like a failure. I was committed to make it work, and even quit a successful career with a national cosmetics firm to take this job within the white concrete walls so I could be closer to home. At age twenty-three, I left home and got married. Five years later, I was divorced. I didn't expect the solitude and silence of living by myself in an apartment. For the first time in my life, I felt alone.

For months I cried myself to sleep and called out to God to let me know he was there. One of my aunts and my godmother were both nuns. My aunt used to tell me, 'Jesus is your brother. Just talk to him like he's your brother.' I always felt like the Lord was part of me and my life. He was reachable and accessible. Until now. I felt far away from him, and my Catholic guilt only compounded the feeling. 'Where are you? Show me where you are in my life.' Did he still hear my prayers? I sure didn't get any response. Only deafening silence.

Running became my focus. Running away from the past. Running toward a new life. Five days a week, five miles a day. In three weeks, I planned to cross the finish line of a biathlon and make a fresh start in my life. I had been training a full year for that milestone date.

The ringing phone at my desk startled me.

'Hello. This is Julie.'

'Hi. Welcome back,' the cheerful voice of my big sister greeted me.

'Hi, Tammy. How are you?' I glanced at my desk clock. *It's already after six.*

'I'm fine. How was your trip to Mexico?'

'Incredible! I've got so much to tell you, but I'm piled under at work right now.' Balancing the receiver between my shoulder and my ear, I put the unopened letters back into the inbox.

'Why don't you come over for dinner tonight? I can't wait to hear all your stories.'

'That sounds great. Are you sure?'

'Of course!'

'Okay. I need to run to the mall for some moisturizer. I'm so sunburned. I'll be at your place a little after seven. Okay?'

'That's fine. I'll see ya then.'

After hanging up the phone, I picked up my purse and

walked to the door. I looked at the pile of papers on my desk and thought, *Tomorrow I'll get organized. There's always tomorrow.* I closed the office door. Then I drove thirty minutes to the mall in Lombard, a western suburb of Chicago.

I bought some moisturizer at one of the department stores and hopped back into my white Mazda MX3, nicknamed 'ET' by my dad because the headlights made him think of ET's eyes. I looked at my watch: 6:55. I'd promised my sister that I'd be there around 7:00. *I'll just be a little late. She'll understand. No need to hurry.*

I turned on the car and headed out of the mall's parking lot. Then, in the simple act of turning left, my life changed forever. I never saw the teenage boy barrel through the red light in his car.

CHAPTER THREE

THE HALLWAY OF LIGHT: VISITING HEAVEN

I am alone.

But not afraid.

I'm standing in the middle of a large, round area engulfed in clear daylight. There is no color, only shades of white. There are no corners, shadows or darkness. I see only round walls of pure light, not blinding light like the sun. I don't know how I got here. The room reminds me of a spacious foyer of an enormous mansion – a place to wait before meeting others for a guided tour. Am I waiting for someone? I look around. Even though the area appears to be part of a larger structure, I don't observe any ceilings. The spaciousness evokes a sense of freedom without constraints or limits. It's not hazy or foggy. Everything is just pure. Clear. Clean. Although this place is unlike anything I know, I am comfortable in its strangeness. I experience an immediate sense of familiarity – not one of déjà vu, for I have never been here before, but rather an innate certainty that this place is where I should be. The place where I belong. It's home.

Everything is silent. No birds. No background noises. No music. Not even a distant hum of anything. I continue to stand in the brilliance and stillness of silence. I exist alone, unafraid and at peace.

Soon I begin to feel restless, as if I'm supposed to leave this room and go to a different place. I turn my head to the left and see an intense white light that outlines the walls and floors of an adjacent hallway. This streaming light is much brighter than the clear light of the round space.

Even though my body doesn't physically move, I'm facing the hallway. It's like a sequence frame from a movie – one second I'm in the middle of this round room, and the next second I'm in front of the hallway. How powerful to be so close to this river of brilliant light that flows away from the round room. The hallway looks long and narrow, and I can't see an end to it. On each side of the hallway, the light streams up the walls like an upside-down waterfall. I notice no ceilings exist in the narrow corridor either.

The streaming light beckons me to enter. Like a moth, I have an inner urgency to go to that light source. I quickly assess the narrowness of the entry and think, 'It's a good thing I'm small enough to squeeze through there.' Every part of me wants to become a part of this light. I know it's a pathway that will bring me to where I'm ultimately supposed to be.

Without hesitation, I'm ready to follow the gentle current and discover where it will take me. I am about to step into the light when I sense the presence of others behind me. Once again, I don't feel myself turning as I look into the soft, wrinkled faces of my two grandmothers, Gram, my mom's mom, and Grandma Sue, my dad's mom. How did they get here? Is this who I'm waiting for? I glance behind them to see if they came from a different entrance, but the space is too vast to determine. It's great to see them again. But they're dead. At that moment, I realize that I must be dead, too. But I don't feel dead. In fact, I've never felt more alive. This must be part of heaven. It must be the

21

waiting area. Wow! I'm in heaven! This all makes sense now. I have no idea what happened to bring me here, but I'm happy to be here. I am not afraid to be dead. I feel such complete peace.

I look at my grandmothers, eager to communicate with them. I'm glad that they are the ones sent to meet me and welcome me to heaven. They look the same as I remember them – even Gram's soft grey hair looks coifed. She had her hair done often. There's so much I want to ask them. Suddenly, they are right in front of me even though they didn't move. They really look terrific.

It was only months ago that Gram had died. I last saw Gram at her house on the night she died. Thanks to the local hospice, Gram was able to say her last good-byes to the family that night in the comfort and privacy of her home. Late into the evening, we all stayed by Gram's side. My Aunt Joanne called and wanted to be with Gram; however, she could not bring her small daughter Lauren. I offered to go over to her home and baby-sit. It was only right that Aunt Joanne should have the opportunity to say good-bye to her own mother. At 3:00 a.m., Lauren woke up in her crib and started sobbing inconsolably. I ran to Lauren's room and picked her up. Minutes later, the phone rang. Mom told me Gram just passed away. I felt her absence in my heart and instantly missed my special friend. But now, I am with her. She and Grandma Sue look healthy and happy. Grandma Sue has her hand on Gram's shoulder. They both are smiling at me. I am surprised that I don't feel compelled to run up and give them a huge hug.

Even though my grandmothers appear the same, I know they are not who they once were. They no longer seem physical. They are spiritual beings. I sense that I'm different than they are. I still feel physical. For the first time in heaven, I look down and discover that I still have a physical body, and it's broken. Something is terribly wrong. I don't know how I know that I'm not okay, but I just know. Everything about me feels heavy. I don't think I belong here, but I want to stay here forever. I must go into the streaming light. I have to stay. I want my grandmothers to go with me through that hallway.

I sense that my grandmothers want to tell me something. I smile. With her hand still on Gram's shoulder, Grandma Sue smiles back. I convey my thoughts to them: 'You both look great, and you're so healthy! I'm glad you are happy.' I lift my right arm and motion them toward me and say through my thoughts, 'Okay. Come on, girls, let's go!' I'm ready and determined to turn toward the river of light in the hallway. I know that if I go through that hallway, I will reach the ultimate place I'm supposed to be.

Gram gently but firmly conveys her thoughts: 'You can't follow us. You have to go back.'

For the first time in heaven, I am afraid. Broken peace. I don't want to go back. I can't go back. I sweep my right hand across the left side of my body and plead with them, 'But I can't go back. I'm not physically okay.' My despair is palpable. Physical. The heaviness of my humanity feels incongruous in the lightness of heaven. I look down for a moment and then lift my head to look at Gram. A brilliant and intense blue tunnel of light streams from behind Gram's eyes. Endless tunnels. This stained-glass blue color makes a stark contrast against the whiteness of the area. I can't look away from those piercing blue eyes.

As this penetrating light surrounds me, I am shocked by its physical warmth. I feel as if it is gathering me in its arms to comfort me and to reassure me that everything will be okay. I also sense that if I walk into this blue light it will lead to eternity, the same path as the narrow hallway. I experience an immediate sense of humbleness, awe, and peace; I have never felt such pure love. I can't stop staring into this light. I don't even squint. I merely accept this overwhelming gift of grace as I sense the presence of the Lord's holiness. Part of me wants to throw myself on the ground, but I can't move my legs. All I can do is stare at this streaming light and feel a tangible peace wash through my body.

'Your body will heal,' Gram says. The conveyed voice is one of absolute authority. Beyond dispute. I know that the Lord has sent my grandmothers as angelic messengers to comfort, console, and direct me with his words. I believe and trust that God will heal my body. I feel the same peace at that moment as I did when I first arrived. I know everything will be okay.

With the same brilliant light in her eyes, Gram says, 'Go back and be happy.'

I know that I must return. I don't belong here yet. It isn't my time to be in heaven. I have to go back and finish my life and find happiness. God must have a reason and purpose for me not to stay. I trust him. I feel such hope. I feel such unconditional love. I know that whatever happens I will be okay. My faith is no longer 'blind.' I experience the permeating and healing warmth of God's boundless love and grace. His message, *Go back and be happy*, encompasses my fears, as a parent wraps his shivering child into a warm blanket. It was like God took that big blanket and said, 'Here you go.' I feel as if he put his arms around me and wrapped me in that blanket and said, 'It's going to be okay, Julie. I'm with you. Always with you.'

How humbling and reassuring to realize that he personally cares. Nothing can separate me from God's love. I must obey. I must go back.

CHAPTER FOUR

THE AFTERMATH: WAKING UP FROM A COMA

My body popped and shuddered. I opened my eyes. I couldn't see. The brightness was blinding, not welcoming like the light in heaven. *Where am I? Whose body is this? It doesn't even feel like mine.* I was alone. I was back.

My left arm lay limp. Lying still, I turned my head and looked around the room. Everything seemed blurry and out of focus. *This is weird. I see two of everything. What happened to my 20/20 vision? Everything was clear in heaven. Looks like a hospital. Why can't I feel or move my left side?* Peering down at my left arm, I thought, *Wake up, arm! You have to move now.* But it remained motionless. My body parts felt fragmented and disconnected, like they were trapped inside a Picasso painting. Lifting my right arm, I discovered a call button attached to the bed rail. *I need to find out what's going on.* Somehow, I knew that I was supposed to press the red button. Seconds later, a surprised nurse ran into my room. 'You're awake!' she exclaimed. Three other nurses rushed to my side. They sounded like chattering geese. I couldn't process all of their words at the same time.

In a hoarse whisper I asked, 'What happened?' I was surprised that my throat hurt when I spoke, as if I had a severe case of strep throat. I couldn't catch a full breath.

I felt as if my body had a hidden leak of air, like a bicycle tire, but I couldn't pump air back inside. *My voice sounds different.* I lifted my right hand to my neck and felt a large indentation and loose skin that covered it. *What is this? Why is there a hole in my neck?*

A nurse leaned close to my face and enunciated very slowly, as if she thought I would have problems understanding her, 'You were in a really bad car accident, Julie. A teenager ran a red light and hit your car. You're at Marianjoy in Wheaton. It's a rehabilitation hospital. The doctors took you off the respirator and put a tracheotomy tube in your throat so you could breathe. That's why you feel that bumpy hole there. It's a miracle you even woke up.'

Car accident? Respirator? A miracle I woke up? Do my parents know?

Anxious for an answer, I forced myself to speak, 'Did someone call my mom and dad?' I discovered that the pain in my throat was less intense when I pressed the place of the incision with my right hand to talk.

'Yes,' she said. 'Your parents know, and they'll be here soon.'

'How's my yellow Toyota?' *Why in the world did I just say that? I've never even driven a yellow Toyota!*

'I don't know about that. But do you remember the date of your accident?'

I shook my head in response. *I can't even remember an accident. How could I know the date?*

'Your accident was on 10 May 1993,' the nurse said and then asked, 'Do you want us to call your husband?'

'No. I'm divorced.' *Oh, good, I remembered something. A clue to my past.*

'You're right,' the nurse replied. *Then why did you ask me if you already knew?*

'Julie, who is the President of the United States?'

Oh, checking to see what else I can remember. Can't you just talk to me? I have so many questions.

'Nixon?' I imagined the *Jeopardy* music clicking in my head as I pressed the buzzer to win the round. As the nurse's facial expression confirmed I wasn't correct, I imagined Alex Trebek's voice: 'I'm sorry, Julie. That is the wrong answer.'

'Actually, Bill Clinton is the president, but you're right about Nixon. He once was president – a few decades ago.'

I felt overwhelmed and confused. Talking exhausted me. Thinking exhausted me. Being alive exhausted me. The nurse's questions seemed too complicated. I turned my head the other way on the pillow. Fatigue wrapped its heavy weights around my consciousness, lulling me to go back to sleep.

'Honey, you just rest,' the nurse assured me. 'You have an extremely severe brain stem injury, and you've been in a coma for four weeks.'

I've been in a coma for four weeks? Extremely severe brain stem injury? What is a brain stem? Then came the shocking part.

'By the way,' the nurse added, as she adjusted my pillow, 'Don't try to get out of bed. You won't be able to walk. You're paralyzed on your left side.'

The nurses then left the room in a flurry of excitement, chattering as they walked down the hallway, 'I can't believe she's awake! She's even talking! I'll let the doctor know right away.'

I stared at the white ceiling and the fluorescent lights above my bed. *Oh, by the way, you're paralyzed? What am I supposed to say: 'Thanks for letting me know?' What does it even feel like to be paralyzed? I'm a runner, training for a biathlon. Yes, that's right. I'm a runner. I remember how it feels to stride across a paved surface in cushioned running shoes. My muscles have to still be strong. I ran five miles five days a week and bicycled even more. I have very strong legs. There's no way that these legs can't hold me up to stand. I just have to see what that nurse was talking about.*

With great effort, I pulled myself up into a wobbly sitting position. I couldn't get my balance, but I felt encouraged enough to try. *Good. I can sit, and if I can sit, I can stand.* As an athlete, I had done sit-ups regularly and my abdominals were strong. Somehow, I managed to lower the side rail and pulled my left leg over with my right arm. As both legs dangled from the bed, I felt something bulky and uncomfortable under my gown. Patting the side of my right hip, I felt the crunch of plastic. Reality hit. *A diaper. I'm in a diaper!* I slid off the bed and tried to stand.

My legs collapsed under the weight of my body. Hearing the commotion, the chattering geese ran back into my room. 'Thank God you didn't hit your head,' the same nurse exclaimed. 'Julie, you don't understand. You have an extremely severe brain stem injury, and you can't walk. Look, here's the doctor. He'll explain everything to you.'

I wanted to scream, but I remained quiet in my humiliation as the nurses lifted my limp body off the floor and put me back into bed. *All I wanted was to see what it felt like to be paralyzed. Now I understand. I really am paralyzed. I'm an athlete, and I can't even stand up. This is great, God. Really great. You sent me back here, and I can't even stand. My body is broken.*

A doctor stood by my bedside. 'Julie, the nurse is right. You have a severe brain stem injury. No one expected you to wake up from your coma. Statistically you shouldn't be here, since 96 per cent of people with your condition pass away.' As the doctor talked, he examined me. He shone a bright light into my eyes, and I squinted. 'Your left pupil is completely blown. It doesn't even react to the light.' He listened to my breathing with a stethoscope. 'Are you seeing double?' he asked. I nodded. 'We'll make arrangements to have a patch put over that eye. Any pain?' I shook my head. 'You understand that you're paralyzed, right?' I nodded. 'I'm sorry that happened to you. We'll do the best we can here to help you rehabilitate, but you have to be realistic in your expectations. The brain stem is the central command center for your body, controlling breathing, pulse and body movements. Your brain stem is extremely damaged.' He crossed his arms over his chest. 'The fact that you woke up defies medical realities. This is a real miracle. Do you have any questions for me?'

I shook my head. I was still in shock from hearing the gloomy medical statistics and prognosis. I didn't have the energy to think of a question, much less put it into words.

'I'll continue to check up on you throughout your stay,' the doctor said, and left the room.

The chatty nurse approached my bed. 'Julie, we need to strap you in so you won't hurt yourself.' She tightened a 'seatbelt' across my motionless body. 'It's for your own protection.' I acquiesced. What choice did I have? Where would I go anyway? The nurses left the room.

I sobbed. *God, what am I supposed to do now?*

Trapped in my body and strapped in my bed, I tried to recapture the indescribable peace that I found in heaven's light. I bit my bottom lip as it quivered, and I tasted the salty residue of my tears. *Why can't I just go back to heaven, God? I felt so close to you. Everything was peaceful. I know that verse in Psalm 46 says, 'Be still and know I'm God.' But did I have to become paralyzed to be still and know you? Now you seem so far away. I cannot see or feel the light here*

– only the buzzing fluorescent light above my bed. Why can't I feel the light? I don't belong here. I want to be with you in the light. Please take me back there.

As a child, I played with magnetic dolls and would laugh when I attached the head to the arm or the leg to the shoulder. Now, I was the magnetic doll, disjointed and disconnected from my own body. Exhausted from waking up and being alive, I fell asleep.

CHAPTER FIVE

EVERYDAY LESSONS:
SQUEEZING TOOTHPASTE

Someone tapped at the door. I opened my eyes: I saw my parents. They looked the same, yet different – tired and older. My dad's premature grey hair looked more grey. His six-foot-six-inch frame appeared stooped, as if he had been carrying an armload of bricks. My mom's blue eyes were faded like an old pair of worn-out Levi jeans. They rushed to my bed and started to cry. I wanted to jump up and give them a hug from my heart.

'Hi,' I whispered as I tried to lift my right hand in an effort to wave, but it felt too heavy to move.

Dad's face melted into a huge smile. He leaned over the bed to hug me and shouted, 'Our prayers have been answered! Thank you, God!'

I was surprised to hear my dad express these emotional thoughts. I wanted to hug him back – the same way as when I was a kid. My dad would scoop me up in his strong arms to hug me and I felt protected. Now, I couldn't even lift my arms to fling them around his neck.

Dad's hug exuded unrestrained joy at seeing me again – just like the hug he gave me at the Christmas tree farm when I was eight years old and lost sight of him. Choosing the Christmas tree with Dad was an annual tradition. That year my sister Tammy stayed home because she was sick.

Even though I felt bad for her, I was secretly happy that this special outing would just be Dad and me. I've always been a daddy's girl, and I cherished any moment I could spend alone with him. Dad and I wandered through the maze of trees displayed. Rows and rows of evergreens hovered high above us in the moonlight.

Suddenly, I looked around, and I couldn't find my dad. The dangling spotlights cast scary shadows around the trees. I yelled, 'Dad!' Then, out of nowhere, I felt my dad's huge hug. He had always been close by. From my hospital bed, I wanted to shout, *Dad! Everything's okay now that you're here*. All I had the energy to do was to smile.

Mom kissed me on the cheek and brushed back my hair. 'Julie,' she whispered, 'I knew you'd be okay.' At this moment I appreciated her emotional restraint. Mom handled even the most traumatic situations without outbursts. She has the toughness and tenacity of a pit bull and the gentleness of Aunt Bea from *The Andy Griffith Show*. Mom possesses the ability to assess a situation and know what needs to be done without drama. She quietly reached for my hand to hold onto me. This small act of reassurance empowered me.

After the initial rush of emotion, words didn't come easily to any of us. I had so much that I wanted to ask and say. *What happened to me? I'm so sorry about all of this. By the way, I saw your moms in heaven, and they look great!* But words didn't come. I didn't have the strength to deal with anything, especially putting my feelings into words. At that moment, I just wanted to be with my parents, see them smile and hear them speak.

'I'm sorry we weren't with you when you woke up,' Mom said, combing her fingers through my hair to brush it back. That felt good. 'We've tried to have someone with you as much as possible. I can't believe you woke up the one time someone wasn't here.'

The talkative nurse returned to my room. 'What an exciting morning. Let's change your diaper and get you ready.' *What a way to start the day.* My parents left the room to give me, their twenty-nine-year-old daughter, some privacy.

As the nurse lifted me up and removed the soiled diaper, I felt humiliation. A stranger was washing my private area and putting a fresh diaper on me. What had my life turned into? I wanted to ask so many questions, but I was fearful of upsetting anyone by asking. I decided not to talk, but rather to assess the situation and let others talk. Listening has always been one of my strongest traits, even as a young student. Others always confided in me, and I never told their secrets. I would just sit and listen.

'Okay, you're all changed and dressed. Now it's time to eat. I brought your breakfast.'

Breakfast? I looked around the room for a tray. *Yeah. I guess I do feel a little hungry. I wonder what she brought. That's strange. I don't smell bacon or pancakes or anything.*

'Here we go. I'll attach this to your tube.'

Attach what to what tube? Why is she holding a jar of paste?

The nurse lifted my gown and skillfully connected plastic tubes from the jar into the plug that was sticking out of my stomach. I watched the paste go through the tubes. I didn't chew anything, swallow anything, or taste anything, but somehow I felt full. Very strange.

My parents came back into the room as I was being fed. I was surprised that they didn't react with shock to someone putting food through a tube into their daughter's stomach. They just rubbed my arm and talked to me like all this was part of a normal routine for them to observe. I realized that this was part of their normal routine for the past few weeks, but it was all new to me. Shockingly new.

'Your daughter was talking this morning and answering all sorts of questions, right, honey?' the chattering nurse said as she checked the feeding tube machine.

I had no desire to answer any more questions from that nurse. Actually, I had no desire to talk to anyone, even when a reunion of family and friends gathered in my room later that day. Everything was just overwhelming. I was thankful that I could remember who each person was. My sister Tammy and her husband John. My brother Brett. Aunt Kathy and Uncle Peter. My best friends Sue and Jill and other family members. Many of them were crying. I looked around the room and tried to smile. I didn't want them to be sad. I would never do anything to upset my family and friends. I wished I had the energy to comfort everyone, but I just didn't want to talk. I didn't feel confident enough about what I would say.

What an odd feeling to relieve myself in my diaper as everyone stood around my bed crying and exclaiming how happy they were to see me awake. Everyone kept remarking how amazing it was that I woke up. I just smiled and hid my feeling of despair.

That night, I couldn't sleep, and I couldn't stop crying. I felt like a big open wound, vulnerable and in pain. I longed for the company of all my family and friends. The last time all of us had been together was at Gram's funeral a few months before. *Gram. I miss her. I am homesick for heaven.* Unbearable loneliness throbbed through my body. I felt like I was back at the Christmas tree farm hiding from the scary shadows. *I'll just take some pills. That won't be painful. No mess for anyone to clean up. God didn't want me to come back to this. I feel hopeless, not happy.*

I didn't think of this as suicide. I just thought it was a way to get back to the round room engulfed in white light. I missed the narrow hallway. The only whiteness that surrounded me now was a curtain divider, the sheets under which I was strapped and the drab walls. I fell asleep.

When I woke up around 5:00 a.m., everything was quiet. I was still alone. Like the time after my divorce, I lay in bed and cried, 'Where are you, God?

I couldn't get beyond each minute, discovering something else I could no longer do. With my right hand, I touched the side of my head. *Okay, I have a huge bald spot, and my brain isn't working well. What am I going to do about that?* I touched the scar on my neck. *Okay, my voice isn't working well. What am I going to do about that?* I touched the feeding tube plug in my stomach. *Okay, I'm not able to eat on my own. What am I going to do about that?* I touched my right hip and crunched the plastic diaper. *Okay, I can't go to the bathroom on my own. What am I going to do about that?* I touched my left arm and thigh. *Okay, I am paralyzed. What am I going to do about that?* Then I did the only thing I knew I could do: I cried out to God.

Please help me. I'm still here, even though I don't want to be. Part of me feels really guilty for feeling this way, but I just don't belong here. My body is so broken. It was easier to be dead than to be alive. I'm sorry if this disappoints you. Please bring me back to heaven.

Mom walked into my room. 'Good morning,' she said, kissing me on the forehead. 'I'll be with you for all of your sessions today.'

I looked at her and thought, *Sessions?* I just nodded. I was glad she was with me. I didn't want to feel alone.

Soon an outgoing young man pushed an empty wheelchair into my room. 'Rise and shine. I'm your transporter today. It's time to start your morning therapy sessions. Are you ready?'

Am I ready? Is anyone really ever ready for this kind of life? I just nodded.

'Every day, you'll get a schedule for your sessions. It's up to you to let me know when we go where,' the transporter explained, handing me a piece of paper. 'Here's your schedule for today. Why don't you look it over and tell me where we go?'

I took the paper with my right hand and looked at it. The typed words looked blurry, but I could read them. *I can read! I see two of every word, but I can read!* I pressed my throat and in a hoarse whisper said, 'Physical therapy.' I felt obligated to speak to him. I always followed the rules.

My mom remained silent, but I observed a misting in her eyes as she realized her daughter could not only still read, but speak aloud difficult words.

Even with my double vision, I clearly saw what I was facing. As the transporter rolled me down the long, wide hallway, I noticed that everyone was in a wheelchair. My heart ached for these fellow patients. I didn't like to see anyone suffering. I wished that there were something I could do, but I didn't have the strength. For twenty-nine years, I had been able-bodied. Now I would have to learn how to live in a disabled body with an able mind. *Can I do this?*

He wheeled me into another hallway, where I parked in line behind the other wheelchairs for a physical therapy session. 'It'll be your turn in a few minutes,' he said. I nodded and looked around. I noticed the heavy double doors at the end of the hallway. In a sense, we were all prisoners here, brought together through different circumstances and with different sentences. We were serving our time together. Waiting. All we could do was wait. We had all

36

been stopped at an unexpected red light. Now we waited for the green light so we could move forward again – not along the original route that each of us had planned, but along one that would one day take us beyond the locked, double doors of this hallway. Out of this prison and back into the world that I knew.

Mom stayed close to my side as I, slumped in my wheelchair. My abdominal muscles, once strong, had atrophied to a point at which I could barely hold myself upright. The dizziness further compounded the challenge of even sitting in a wheelchair.

When it was my turn, a female physical therapist called my name. As Mom pushed my wheelchair into the room, I noticed the therapists were around my age. 'Julie,' one of the therapists said, 'you woke up. That's amazing! We'll be able to get a lot done now.' She attached a belt around my waist, pulled me out of my wheelchair, and gently laid me down onto the thick, blue floor mat. 'I want to help strengthen your muscles to teach them how to stand and move again.' My left side lay limp, unable even to help in the stretching process.

I nodded my head, eager to hear more. *She thinks I will stand and move again.* Those words were full of promise. I was ready to work hard for my recovery. I was an athlete.

'You suffered a severe brain stem injury, which basically shut down the communication from your brain to the left side of your body. We're trying to teach the brain how to talk to your left side again. Makes sense?'

I nodded. *My brain can't talk to my body? Will it ever?*

The therapist moved my left leg into different positions, trying to warm up the atrophied muscles. How strange it was to watch her bend my leg and not to feel a thing. It was like watching someone else's workout in a mirror. I saw the motions, which didn't connect to any sensations in my own body.

'Okay, I'm going to put you on what's called a slant board. It will help you get used to the feeling of standing again. Don't worry, we won't let you fall. Is it okay if I put you on it now?' the therapist asked.

I nodded, eager to do whatever it would take to stand and walk again. She and another therapist placed me on a flat board with a cushioned shelf on the bottom. My feet pressed against this shelf as the two lifted the board to elevate my head. As my body was lifted six inches above the floor, I panicked. *I'm not ready for this.* I felt nauseous from the vertical movement. I was used to being horizontal. Sensing my fear, the therapists gently lowered my body back to the mat. *How can this body heal?*

Mom knelt by my side and wiped my tears. 'It's okay, Julie. This is only your first day awake. You'll learn.' The therapists helped me back into the wheelchair. My session was over. I was exhausted, frightened and overwhelmed.

The transporter returned and asked me to read the sheet. 'Which therapy is next?'

Biting my lip, I read the itinerary and answered in a whisper, 'Speech.'

He wheeled me down the hallway to another therapy room, where I met my speech therapist. She appeared quite young. Brushing back her brown cropped hair with bangs, she explained that my brain was taking longer to make the connection to think and speak. 'It's probably hard to find all the words for your feelings, right?'

I nodded. *Yes! I'm frustrated not being able to remember the right words. But mostly, I'm just afraid to speak. I'm afraid of how hopeless I feel and how I sound.* The girl who was voted 'Most Talkative' in eighth grade now sat in silence with a speech therapist.

My tongue felt thick and displaced, and I couldn't always make it work. Since tongue movement is controlled by the last cranial nerve of the brain, learning to speak again was difficult. I had so much going through my mind at high speed, and I didn't have the energy or the ability to express everything. The therapist handed me a piece of paper. 'Can you read this short paragraph?' she asked.

'Yes,' I whispered. Once again, I felt an obligation to speak since this felt like a type of class. With much effort I expressed my thoughts. 'But everything is moving.' I couldn't stop the highway of words that whizzed by on the page, but I managed to read.

'Good job,' she said, and then asked me to name objects and recite the days of the week. I barely had enough energy even to whisper. My therapist sensed my frustration and commented, 'Your severe brain stem injury and tracheotomy have affected your ability to speak. Don't expect too much of yourself.' Had I not been so emotionally overwhelmed, perhaps I would have interpreted her comments as those that just applied to the moment, not to my future. But I was ultra sensitive. *Don't expect much? How can you say that to me? I expect more than you could ever imagine. My body will heal! Don't you dare try to steal my hope away. That's all I have to get me through each minute of my life.*

'Try to sip some orange juice,' the therapist said, holding a plastic cup with a straw inside.

I put my lips atop the straw. That action reminded me how to sip through the straw and swallow.

'Great job,' the therapist said. 'You're able to swallow.'

Soon the transporter returned. 'Okay, where to next?' he asked, handing me the paper with my schedule.

'Occu.' I paused, then continued with a slight stutter, 'Occupational therapy.'

'Well, then, it's off to OT. That will be back in your room.' He wheeled me down the hallway and to my room. I remained in my wheelchair, slumped to the side in exhaustion.

'Hi, Julie, I'm Sheila, your occupational therapist. I want to help you relearn how to take care of yourself. We'll work on toilet training, personal grooming, writing and improving motor skills.'

I sighed. I could physically do very few things. I didn't even want to think about the logistics of toilet training, even though I was eager to stop wearing wet diapers.

'I brought some paper and a pen so you can try to write,' Sheila said. She pushed the moveable hospital tray to my wheelchair and lowered the table.

She helped position the pen in my right hand and said, 'There, you should be able to write just fine with a little practice. Good thing your right side isn't paralyzed.'

'But I'm left-handed,' I whispered. Holding something in my right hand just felt weird. *Great. My whole life I've been a lefty. Now I have to learn how to write with my right hand.* I gripped the pen and tried to write my name. *Even a monkey's scribbling looks better than this.* I felt like a failure. I couldn't even complete the simple task of writing my name.

'That's okay, Julie,' Sheila said. 'I'll work with you. Don't worry.'

I appreciated her encouragement and realized that Sheila would be a key person in preparing me for life out of this rehabilitation facility.

'Let's wheel you into the bathroom and brush your teeth,' Sheila said.

With my right hand, I placed the toothbrush onto the edge of the sink. Then, I grabbed the toothpaste and flipped open the top. I squeezed, aimed, fired and missed. A glob of toothpaste splattered into the sink.

'That's okay, Julie,' Sheila cheered me along. 'Just try it again.'

'Can I brush with my fingers?' Whenever I forgot to pack my toothbrush for sleepovers as a child, I would just use my pointer finger.

'No,' Sheila smiled and sternly replied, 'You're not a kid anymore. Just keep trying.'

I know I'm not a kid, but I'm not even able to function like a toddler. I've got to figure this out. This is something I will have to do every day for the rest of my life. I'm an accountant. There has to be a logical way to make it work.

'Come on, Julie. Keep trying. You're almost there.'

Finally, I put the tube even closer to the toothbrush and squeezed a dab out instead of a glob. It worked. Then came the hard part: I had to maneuver the toothbrush with my right hand. It felt so awkward, like driving on the left side of the road. It was hard to steer, but I did it. That was a good feeling. I accomplished an everyday task, and I was exhausted. That is the most difficult part about waking up from a coma. Even though my body had been asleep for a long period of time, I didn't feel very rested.

Sheila and Mom helped transfer me back into my bed. It had been a busy first morning. Mom helped relax me by rubbing my right arm, something she knew I loved. On those nights when I was sick as a child, Mom would rub my arms to help me fall asleep. She would gently massage my arms and glide her fingertips across the inside of my elbow. 'Just relax, Julie. Just relax. It's going to be okay.' Those same motions and words once again helped calm me as an adult.

All I could think about was how difficult my life had become. As Mom rubbed my arm, I recalled her words during my childhood when I would come home from school overwhelmed by antics on the playground. 'It's just too hard!' I would complain. Each time I reached that point, we would sit at the kitchen table and Mom would always say, 'It was never meant to be easy here. This is our place of work. We get our gift of peace when we get to heaven.' If I could only tell Mom how true her words were. I missed the gift of peace I found in heaven.

My sister Tammy came in the room. 'I'll be back later tonight,' Mom said, and kissed my forehead. I nodded.

A nurse walked in. 'Time to eat, Julie.' *Lunch menu: paste again*. After my busy morning, I appreciated not having to lift a fork. While I 'ate,' Tammy arranged items on my dresser and tables. Like my mom, she had the gift of domesticity. As a child, Tammy always chose to bake and clean with Mom. I always chose to run wild and do cartwheels in the backyard. Fearless and boundless at age four, I ran around the neighborhood without letting my parents know. Even when my mom asked Dad to build a fence in the backyard so I wouldn't wander out, I kept running. No one could lasso my free spirit with the drudgery of being still. Until now.

After my lunch and hour-long nap, my transporter appeared. 'I'm back.' He handed me my afternoon schedule for even more therapy sessions. *Don't I even get a break here?* Tammy went to the sessions with me. Once again, the physical therapists placed me on the slant board and lifted my body from the floor. With mental resolve, I let them lift me higher. I fought the nausea. I fought the dizziness. I fought back the tears.

Later that day, I had occupational therapy again. Sheila said, 'Julie, try to wash your face by yourself in the bathroom.'

Wash my face by myself. Can I do that? She helped me wheel myself into the bathroom. I used my right hand to steer. The bar of soap was slippery and kept falling into the sink.

I can't do this! I can't believe I'm not even able to wash my own face!

Frustrated, I threw everything out of the bathroom and erupted into sobs. Sheila calmly said, 'Okay, Julie, I can see you had a fit here. Just go wheel yourself out of the bathroom and let's pick up everything.'

I can't even wheel myself without bumping into anything.

Sheila reassured me: 'Julie, You can do this. It's hard work, but you're up to it.' She knelt on the floor and handed the washcloth and soap to me. 'Try it again.'

Okay. She's seen this before. She knows I can do it. Just try it again. This time, I held the soap for a few seconds until it once again tumbled into the sink.

When Mom returned that evening, she said, 'Tammy and I are going to give you a shower tonight.'

Tammy and Mom wheeled me into a large shower room that was down the hall. Long hoses hung from the ceiling. I felt like I was in a spinning carwash, since my vertigo was acute. *They let you get the wheelchairs wet?*

Mom and Tammy scrubbed my body with a washcloth and soap. I sat motionless in my wheelchair. Naked and vulnerable. Tammy joked, 'Julie, if you ever doubted that I love you, this should cinch it.' I summoned a smile, appreciative, yet silent in my humiliation and inability to even hold onto the bar of soap.

After visiting hours were over, my family and friends left. The night nurse changed my diaper, put a gown on me, and strapped me in bed. Lying there alone, unable to sleep, I thought, *What if there's a fire? How will I get out of the building? I'm strapped in. I won't be able to crawl to safety.*

I prayed. *God. What do you have planned for me? Why did you send me back? I am so overwhelmed.* My tears soaked the pillow as I turned my head to fall asleep.

The tears and sense of helplessness obstructed my progress. I sobbed through each therapy session. I cried when the nurses strapped me in bed. My only consolation each day was the distinct memory of my special visit in heaven. What a gift to be able to close my eyes and relive the experience in the light. I remember those times as rainbow moments, when heaven's light refracted a prism through my tears. God's rainbow. His visible reminder that he will always be there through the storms. At night, I clung to this hope and my faith in God, but during the day I cried. Within a few days, the doctor decided to intervene.

A nurse held a tiny plastic cup with a pill inside. I just stared at it. Anti-depressants? Who would ever think that I, always the happy one, Julie Papievis, would be diagnosed as depressed?

Mom stood by my bed. She stroked my hair. 'It's okay. The doctors told us if you keep crying in therapy so much, they won't be able to help you. You'd have to go home. You need to take this pill.'

I nodded. 'Take a sip of some water,' the nurse said, putting the pill in my mouth.

At that moment, I swallowed any speck of pride that remained inside of me. *God, I am humbled beyond words. Your message was 'Go back and be happy.' These people think I'm depressed. I don't want to disappoint you. But I needed help.*

The tiny pill numbed me, like 'white noise,' blocking out the background distractions of emotion. That night, they strapped my body and my feelings in bed. I didn't cry.

During the next few days, I made significant progress in my therapy sessions. My emotions were under control, and I could physically focus on what needed to be done. In speech therapy, I began to have the courage to hear my voice. I was too social a person to be afraid to speak with others. Communication was important to me. I also made huge strides in occupational therapy. Although I was months away from not needing a diaper, my mind was starting to communicate with my bowels and bladder as to what they should be doing. Potty training as an adult is a humiliating experience. Yet, it was something that I had to learn how to do again. Sheila, my occupational therapist, helped me learn how to balance on the toilet and to hold onto the rail.

One morning, a nurse came in the room and said, 'You're scheduled for surgery tomorrow to remove the stomach tube. You'll be eating on your own after that.' Everything seemed to be happening so fast. Too fast. I had only been awake for less than two weeks.

On the morning of my surgery, I was wheeled into an ambulance. Lying on the stretcher, with my mom holding my hand, I thought, I'm so glad that you're with me, Mom. I'm really scared.

I was wheeled into the trauma center of a hospital. 'Where are we?' I asked, looking around.

'We're at Loyola,' Mom answered. 'This is where you were brought after your accident.'

The life-changing accident that I can't even remember.

While waiting in the hospital on my stretcher, I shook.

'What's wrong? Are you cold?' Mom asked as she brushed back my blond hair with her hand.

'When is this going to be over?' I whispered.

'The procedure shouldn't take very long,' she answered. But Mom knew. I wasn't only talking about that day's surgery but about the whole recovery process. I wanted to fast forward my life to a point in the future when I would be well again. Looking at my mom, I realized that I wasn't the only one affected by the accident.

A female doctor approached my stretcher. Petite and muscular, she spoke in a British accent. 'Hello, Julie. I'm Dr Wendy Marshall, and I'll be performing the procedure today. I was the chief trauma doctor on duty the time of your accident. I can't believe you're alive. This is amazing! You weren't even supposed to live through the night, much less wake up and get a feeding tube removed. You should know something: people don't survive such severe brain stem injuries as yours. This is a miracle.'

In my compromised state, I wasn't able to fully grasp the miraculous reality of my progress. I was only able to face the reality of each day's demands.

Due to the extent of my injury, the doctors could not administer general anesthesia. They did not want to put me back into a state of deep unconsciousness. Fully awake in the operating room, I kept gagging on the tubes being removed through my esophagus. It was like a scene from a magic show when a magician keeps pulling endless scarves out of his sleeve. Finally, the procedure ended, and Dr Marshall said, 'Okay, Julie, you're all set. I still can't believe it. You're alive.'

You can't believe it? I can't believe that I just had three tubes pulled out of my throat. I was exhausted, and my throat hurt.

The next morning, Mom came to my room early. She wanted to be with me during my first meal. That day, I would learn how to chew and swallow food. After the nurse performed the morning routine, she wheeled me into the hallway. For each meal, I would have to eat in the hallway so the nurses could be close in case I started choking.

Mom scooped some Jell-O into a spoon and brought it to my lips. By instinct, I opened my mouth. For a moment, the orange Jell-O jiggled on my tongue. It felt odd not to have a sense of taste. The brain injury took that away from me as well. I could only feel the texture of the food.

But the experience triggered a childhood memory. I was nine years old again, sitting in my bed after a bad bout of strep throat. Mom laid a tray of Jell-O, soup, and soda on my night stand. 'Julie, you need to eat. I know your throat hurts. This will help.' Trusting my mom, I scooped some Jell-O onto my spoon, chewed, and swallowed. I was okay.

Now, balancing the orange Jell-O on my tongue, I was afraid. What if I choke? Sensing my uncertainty, Mom touched my throat and said, 'Come on, Julie, you can chew and swallow. You can do it.'

Mom was right. I didn't choke. My wheelchair became my high chair. Mom tucked a napkin in my gown like a baby bib for my meals. Then she lifted the fork, and I held her arm with my right hand as she guided the food to my mouth. Looking at her face, I felt an overwhelming sense of unconditional love. Yet at the same time, I couldn't believe the new reality of my life: an adult child in need of diapers who gets spoon-fed by her mother. Will I become an adult again? Will I ever become me again?

CHAPTER SIX

FINDING FOCUS: A NEW REALITY

With my depression medically under control, everyone felt that I was ready for my first daytime outing – a visit to my parents' home to celebrate Father's Day. This was the end of the second week after awakening from the coma. In anticipation of my return, Dad, a carpenter, stayed up all night to build an elaborate handicap access ramp from the driveway to the backdoor. The next morning, my parents came to the rehabilitation facility to take me home. They transferred me from the wheelchair to the backseat of the car and buckled me in.

This was my first car ride since the accident. I was afraid. Dad turned on the ignition. The running engine made my stomach feel queasy. I felt claustrophobic, trapped by the fear of what could happen and living with the knowledge of what actually can happen.

As we drove out of the parking lot, Mom sensed something was wrong. 'Are you okay?'

'No,' I moaned. *I can't believe I have to be so afraid to be in a car now.* My life was a fearful box where anything could happen. I felt exposed. My protective layers had been ripped.

The trees and homes blurred. I vomited all over the backseat of their new Buick LeSabre. Dad stopped the car and they cleaned me up. I was like a child again, getting carsick. Mom used to keep an empty coffee can in the car for the family trips. I always got carsick. It was the family joke: 'Do you have the coffee can for Julie?'

When we arrived home, I noticed the handicap ramp. 'What's this for?' I asked.

'Your dad built it,' Mom answered. 'He stayed up all night to build it for you. He did a great job, didn't he?'

As my dad pushed me up the ramp, all I could feel was anger. 'I don't need this ramp,' I said defiantly. 'Dad, you know that. I'm not going to stay in a wheelchair. I will be walking soon.' In my mind, the ramp represented a barrier to recovery, not a gateway. It's not that I didn't appreciate what he did. I was angry at what my body wouldn't let me do.

'Of course you will,' Dad said, patiently pushing the wheelchair through the backdoor. How ironic that I was entering through the backdoor – the same door I stood by one day as a young child with a little suitcase in my hand. My mom had asked, 'Where do you think you're going?' I answered, 'I'm running away.' Mom looked at my suitcase and said, 'Well, if you're leaving, you can't take anything with you. You came into this world with nothing, and you'll leave this house with nothing, too.' Now, I was coming back into this home with nothing.

Tammy was already inside. 'Hi, Julie,' she said, and gently hugged me. Dad wheeled me into the family room. While Mom was busy in the kitchen with Tammy, Dad lifted me onto the couch and placed a pillow behind my back. 'Seems hard to believe the last time you were here was on Mother's Day, May 9th. Remember?'

'The only thing I remember is my friends picking me up at the airport and dropping me off here.' I looked at him, frustrated at myself for not being able to remember.

'Oh, that's okay.' Dad adjusted the pillow behind my

back. 'It meant a lot to Mom for you to be with her then.' He cleared his throat. 'And it means a lot to me that you're here for Father's Day.'

The day was 20 June. At least forty days had passed since my accident. How long must I travel through this unknown wilderness which had become my life? Like the Jews during their exodus in the desert, I too depended on God's daily provision of strength. My manna from him was my distinct memory of my visit in heaven. During those moments of complete despair, I was able to close my eyes and remember the indescribable feeling of peace.

Although I was at my childhood home, I felt out of place. Reminders were everywhere that nothing was the same. I wasn't the same. After my nap, Mom and Tammy couldn't get me out of bed, into the wheelchair and onto the toilet fast enough. I urinated all over the bathroom tile floor. From the bathroom doorway, Dad watched. I felt sorry for him. There was nothing he could do. I wanted to go back to the rehabilitation facility. *I don't belong here yet.*

On the way back, I rode in the front seat of the car. Mom brought along a coffee can.

I settled into my room and welcomed the feeling of familiarity, the place where I belonged for now but not forever.

With the anti-depressant medicine, my sense of humor returned. One day the therapist lifted me out of the wheelchair with a belt and positioned me on the mat. Loosening her grip on the belt, she said, 'Okay, Julie, try it on your own.' I took one step and fell. I was so dizzy. Plopping onto the mat, I joked, 'Okay, who tripped me this time?'

I was able to laugh at myself again, just like the time I was trying out for cheerleading in junior high. In front of the judges, my body and my words got tangled. I started laughing. They started laughing. 'Let's try this again,' I had said back then.

'Let's try this again.' Now I said it as an adult.

My everyday world, however, became a Tilt-a-Whirl ride. I was constantly dizzy with double vision. As children, Tammy and I loved to spin around and around on this ride at the summer carnivals. Laughing, we would get off the Tilt-a-Whirl, bump into each other and sit on the pavement until the twirling stopped. The dizziness went away back then. Now it didn't.

The director of rehabilitation referred me to a developmental optometrist, Dr Neil Margolis. Prior to seeing this doctor, I wore a black patch over my left eye to reduce the double vision. I looked like a blonde pirate. I joked with my dad about my double vision, saying, 'Wow, I have so many visitors! There's two of everyone!'

During the third week after I awoke from the coma, Dad drove me to my first eye appointment. He lifted me out of the wheelchair and put me onto the examination chair. Dr Margolis came in and introduced himself.

I immediately noticed the lyrical quality of his voice. He had grown up in South Africa.

I shook his hand and said, 'It's nice to meet you. I'm Julie Papievis.'

Dr Margolis sat down on the swivel stool and scooted next to my chair. 'May I call you Julie?' he asked.

'Of course.'

'Okay, Julie, I want you to tell me what kind of problems you are having with your vision.'

'Please, just stop my world from spinning,' I whispered.

After performing some vision tests, he made a diagnosis. 'Because of the brain stem injury, your eyes aren't working together as a team to focus on an object. Most likely your fourth nerve and branches of the third nerve were affected. These nerves control the extraocular muscles around the eyeball and coordinate the eye movement and eye teaming as well as pupil responses. I'll order a special prism lens for that. Your extreme sensitivity to bright light is due to the large dilation of your left pupil.' He scooted closer in his swivel chair. 'Unfortunately, Julie, your eye will always stay dilated. You will always have a visual disability. However, we'll design a contact lens to visibly reduce the size of your left pupil and to cut the intensive glare.'

Leaving his office, I wore a temporary lens attached to my glasses. My double vision disappeared. I threw away my pirate patch in a garbage can outside. Although I would need years of vision therapy to help strengthen and retrain my eye muscles to work together as a team, I felt more focused and ready to work on my therapy sessions.

In physical therapy, I was vertical for the first time on the slant board. With the special lens, I didn't feel so intensely dizzy. Being vertical helped facilitate standing on the blue mat as the therapists held a belt around my waist. The therapists cheered as I stood with their help. *Thank you, God! I'm standing!* A few days later, I made even greater strides. I stayed on a stationary bike for one minute. My right leg pedaled for my left leg so it could follow.

Lifting me off the bike, the therapist said, 'Julie, what an accomplishment. You pedaled with your left side. Your brain is starting to remember and communicate.'

I know this really is an accomplishment, God, but it seems like such a long way from what I used to be able to do. Before the accident, I was training for the biathlon at the gym. I would ride ten miles on the bike five days a week. I've gone from ten miles to one minute.

I looked forward each night to visiting hours. One evening, a friend who was a hair stylist came. He said, 'Now that you're up, let's fix your hair. I want to even it out a bit.' I knew the bald spot on my head had something to do with my brain injury, but I wasn't ready to hear the details. Itchy hair was growing back, and my hair felt snarled.

Friends helped me lean back into the bathroom sink so he could rinse my hair. This simple backward movement terrified me. The warm water and shampoo, however, felt relaxing, even though I had a lot of tangles. 'There you go,' my friend said. 'What do you think?' He turned my wheelchair around and lifted me up so I could look in the mirror. During physical therapy, I had glanced at my reflection a few times. On purpose, I would not look at myself for very long. I wasn't ready to see and acknowledge my injured image in the mirror. To express my gratitude, however, I obliged my friend. I looked, really looked. A familiar stranger. No makeup. A scar across the throat. A swollen eye. No sunburn. A very sick girl.

'Thanks. My hair looks great,' was all I could say. I finally understood why everyone looked at me with pity.

After visiting hours each day, I was once again alone. Each day ended with the ritual of a nurse changing my diaper, dressing me in a gown, and strapping me in bed. After the nurse left, I lay still in the silence and the dark. Being alone in a room in this body was an undeniable reality. I was afraid. It was during those alone times, however, that I would try my own physical therapy. 'Move, left hand,' I would whisper. And of course, nothing happened. 'Move left leg.' Nothing. 'Move left foot.' Nothing. Until one evening, everything changed. I felt a piercing tingle through my left toe, the same intense feeling as when a foot falls asleep. 'Move, big toe.' And it did! My left toe moved. Although I had no external feeling on my left side, I felt the 'pins and needles' in my left toe. I believed that God was knitting me back together.

My daily routine started early. Breakfast was served at six. Typically I was awake at five. I would stretch my right arm to touch the photographs of my family and friends on the nightstand. Gently caressing each picture frame, I whispered, 'Good morning.' I felt that in some way, they were with me, and I wasn't alone.

Later that same week, I reached for the telephone early one morning. *I'm going to call my apartment and listen to my answering machine. I want to hear my old voice and check my messages.* I needed to connect to my past. The phone rang.

'Hello,' a familiar voice answered.

'Mom, why are you in my apartment?' I couldn't believe it. Why had my mother answered the phone in my apartment?

'Julie?' She sounded sleepy.

'Yeah. Why are you at my place?'

'At your place?'

'My apartment. What's going on?' *I don't understand. Why would Mom stay over at my place?*

'Julie, we forwarded all of your calls to our house.' She paused and said, 'We moved you out of your apartment after the accident. You remembered your phone number.'

'You what? Moved me out?' I panicked.

'We didn't know if you were ever going to wake up.'

'Then where am I going to live when I get out of here?'

'Of course you can move home with Daddy and me.'

I put down the phone. *God, I don't have a place anymore? I'm homeless? Move back in with Mom and Dad? What is this life you sent me back to? I was a businesswoman with options. What am I now? If you don't mind my asking, God, what are your plans for me?* I didn't even stop to wonder how I had remembered my old phone number and the miracle that represented. My mind was making progress. I was getting used to my daily routine: therapy, more therapy, visiting hours.

One night, my parents and Sue, one of my best friends, were getting me ready for visitors. Dad said, 'Julie, there are so many people out there. We need to wheel you to the lobby. They can't fit in your room.'

'Oh, who all is out there?'

'Family, friends, people from work and your boss.'

'My boss? I don't want him to see me like this.' I was always the impeccable professional, striving to reflect the proper demeanor for my employer and place of employment.

'Don't worry about that. He's already seen you in a coma.' Mom reassured me with a hug.

'Oh, that's right: people did see me like that.'

Mom finished brushing my hair and said, 'She's ready.'

Dad pushed my wheelchair. Sue and Mom walked behind.

Before we got to the lobby's entryway, I said, 'Dad, stop the wheelchair. I want to get out and walk.' *I want to walk into a room like the same old me.*

'Okay,' Dad replied, and helped me stand. Holding me up by my sweat pants, Dad stood close by my side. 'I've got you, Julie.'

Look, God, I'm taking steps. You told me my body would heal. I'm walking!

Dad held me up as I took my first 'shoe steps' as an adult. I was not barefoot on the mat in physical therapy.

A nurse chided, 'You can't take her out of that wheelchair, sir. Those are the rules.'

'Look! She's walking. My daughter's walking! Forget the blasted rules.' Dad remained by my side as I made my grand entry into the waiting area.

Chapter Seven

'STICK OUT YOUR TONGUE': A TASTE OF GRACE

After the stomach tube was removed, I was able to take communion each afternoon with a chaplain. One day he asked, 'Are you mad at God?'

'No, I just wonder how he could let this happen to me.' I looked at my left arm, which lay motionless against my lap.

'What do you think?' The chaplain looked at me with kindness in his eyes.

'Honestly? I think God turned his head for just a second.'

'God never turns his eyes from you,' the chaplain smiled.

I knew that was true. Part of me wanted to share my experience in heaven with this chaplain, but I wasn't ready to talk about it with anyone. *He might not believe me. What if people think I made it all up? They'll think it was the brain injury. I know the truth, though. I have never been more certain about anything in my life.*

Sitting next to my wheelchair, the chaplain asked, 'May I pray with you?'

'Yes,' I nodded. He started reciting the Lord's Prayer, 'Our Father…' This time, I joined him in my scratchy and weak voice. '…who art in heaven, hallowed be thy name. Thy kingdom come. Thy will be done, on earth as it is in heaven. Give us this day our daily bread, and forgive us our trespasses as we forgive those who trespass against us. Lead us not into temptation, but deliver us from evil. For thine is the kingdom, the power, and the glory, now and forever, Amen.'

The chaplain smiled as I finished the prayer on my own. It was the first time I had prayed aloud with someone since the accident.

'Your heart remembered the words,' he said.

I fully understood, 'Our Father, who art in heaven.' I had been there, but I wasn't ready to tell anyone. After the Lord's Prayer, I felt the same peace that I experienced in heaven, an incomprehensible peace.

'I want to tell you something,' I whispered to the chaplain.

'What do you want to tell me?' He pulled his chair closer to my bedside to listen.

'I made a promise to God.' I paused for a moment to think about the impact of what I was about to say. 'I told him that I'd work really hard for my recovery and be in the best physical shape possible, so I can tell everyone his story.' I took a deep breath. 'My body will heal, and everyone will know that it was a gift from God.'

'God knows what is in your heart,' he replied, then asked, 'Would you like to receive communion?'

'Yes,' I answered.

'This is the body of Christ, which has been given up for you. Do this in remembrance of me.' He presented the communion wafer.

'Amen.' I opened my mouth and received God's manna. God's bread of life. *Yes, Lord. I do this and everything in remembrance of you. My body will heal, and everyone will know it was a gift from you.* I didn't know what 'my body will heal' meant. Would I walk again? I did know, however, that I was ready to fill in the blanks and discover what had happened to me.

'Mom, I need to know about the accident.' I leaned forward in my wheelchair. This was during my fourth week at the rehabilitation hospital. With my physical progress, I now wanted to concentrate on my mental well-being, too. I had no memory of one of the biggest events in my life. I felt like I had slept through my own wedding. Everyone else had memories, but I only had questions, and I was ready to ask.

'I was wondering when you would ask,' Mom answered. 'What do you want to know?' She put the laundry basket of clean clothes she had washed at home onto the dresser.

'Everything,' I said, and realized that she needed a more specific question. 'Like, when did you and Dad find out?'

'It was May 10th, the day after Mother's Day. Our neighbors, the Denks, were outside on the patio with us. The weather was nice. The phone rang, and it was the chaplain from Loyola.'

'What did he say?'

'He asked if I have a daughter named Julie. Then said you were in an accident.' She sat on the edge of the bed and smoothed the blanket.

'Did he tell you anything?'

'No. I kept asking if you were okay, but he couldn't discuss a patient's condition over the phone. He just told us to get there as quickly as we could.'

'How did Loyola even know to call you and Dad?'

'They found your two licenses in your purse and called your ex-husband. Thank goodness he was there and gave our number to Loyola.' I remembered how after my divorce I carried around two licenses with me, one with my married name and one with my maiden name. It made the transition easier for various accounts that were still in my married name.

'What did Dad do?'

'He knew something was wrong. I told him, and he ran in the house for the car keys. We didn't know what to think or expect. We just wanted to get to the hospital as fast as we could. Your dad was so nervous that he took the wrong turn on First Avenue.'

'Poor Dad.' I shifted my position in the wheelchair.

'The chaplain was waiting for us at the front desk. He rushed us into a side room and brought in a nurse. We knew then that it must be pretty bad. The nurse started talking in medical terms. Your dad just interrupted and asked, "Is our daughter dead or alive?" I think he stunned her with his abruptness.'

'That's Dad. What did she say?' I felt like I was listening to someone else's story. Not my own.

'She told us you were alive but on life support. Your dad demanded to see you, so she took us to your trauma room.' *I'm not surprised.*

'What did everything look like? What did I look like?'

'The room was small. A lot of tubes were attached to you, and the machines were very loud. But you looked peaceful, like Sleeping Beauty. Your dad ran to your side and shouted, "Wake up, Julie! We're here! It's Mom and Dad! Wake up!" The nurse said you were in a coma. Dad held your hand and prayed.'

Mom took off her glasses and dabbed her eyes with a tissue. *How terrible for both of you.* 'I'm sorry, Mom.'

'Oh, it's just hard to live through that again. I always knew you would ask about it, and you should know.' She pursed her lips and wiped her glasses with the tissue.

'Did you and Dad know that I was going to be okay?'

'We knew in our hearts you would live. I can't explain why.'

'What happened next?' I wanted to know, but didn't want to make Mom cry.

'I needed to call Tammy and your brother, so I left the room. A nurse stopped me in the hall and asked if you had a living will. I told her you're only twenty- nine.'

They must have known I was dying.

Mom put back on her glasses. 'Brett was at a baseball game, but Tammy got there pretty quick. She was worried why you never showed up for dinner. She ran in, screaming, "What happened?" We told her and got into the elevator to head up to the Intensive Care Unit. Just as the doors were about to shut, a hospital worker stuck his hand out to make them reopen. A lifeless person on a stretcher was wheeled in. Tammy looked over and screamed, "It's Julie!"'

How terrible.

'What happened in ICU?' I asked.

'Your dad paced around the hall, trying to get answers. A nurse handed him a plastic bag. It had your personal stuff inside. Dad ran into the waiting room and started pulling things out.'

'What was in it?'

'Your purse, your moisturizer, and,' Mom took a deep breath, 'your torn clothes.' *How horrifying. Somebody had to take off my clothes. I'm glad Mom always told me to wear clean underwear!* 'Your dad just sat in that chair and kept holding up your torn, bloody dress, trying to figure out what had happened. It upset me too much. I had to leave the room.'

The friendly transporter knocked on the door. 'Good morning, Julie. Time for your sessions.'

61

I could not process what the transporter was saying. *This is too much to take in.* 'Can you give us a minute?'

'We'll talk after you get back,' Mom reassured me. The transporter wheeled me out of the room.

My sessions seemed to last forever that day. I wanted to hear more details from my mom. My physical therapist fitted me for a leg brace, since my left leg still dragged. She asked, 'What color would you like?'

'Purple, please.'

'Purple?'

'Yes,' I laughed. 'If I have to wear a brace it might as well look cute.'

The transporter wheeled me back to my room for lunch. I couldn't wait to continue my talk with Mom.

'I'm back.'

'Good. I finished putting away the clothes. How did everything go?' She smiled.

'I was fitted for a brace. It should help me walk.'

'Great. Lunch is here. Let's eat.' She arranged the items on the food tray.

'Mom, I'd rather talk.'

'Let's talk while you eat.' She was forever and will always be a mother, making sure her family is fed.

She scooped my fork into the mashed potatoes. In between bites, I asked, 'What happened in ICU?'

'The doctor spoke to us after the tests. His name was Dr John Shea. He was your neurosurgeon. He said you had a severe brain stem injury so your brain couldn't communicate with the rest of your body. Apparently the brain stem controls breathing, blood pressure and everything else that keeps you alive.' Mom wiped my mouth with the napkin. 'He prepared us for the worst and said there wasn't anything else medically to do for you. He said, "All we can do is pray. Your daughter needs prayers."'

Oh, Mom, I can't even imagine. You had just lost your own mother three months before my accident, and now you had to face the possibility of losing your child.

'I need a nap,' I said. Hearing the facts and seeing the effects on my mother exhausted me, in both a physical and an emotional sense.

Mom rubbed my feet, and I slept for awhile.

When I woke up, Tammy was in the room. It was her turn for a shift. I wanted to ask tons more questions, but I didn't want to upset Tammy, especially after hearing about the elevator incident. Sensing my need to talk, my big sister broke the ice. 'Mom told me you asked about the accident.'

'Yeah.' *There's so much I want to ask you.* I summoned my courage. 'When did you guys decide to move me out of my apartment?'

'A couple of weeks after your accident. Things didn't look too good for you. The family agreed to move you out of there, and I called your landlord.' That is my big sister. She always took charge and made things happen.

'I hope I didn't leave things in a mess.'

'It was spotless,' she laughed, and then turned somber. 'The only thing that seemed out of place was your unpacked suitcase. It sat in the middle of the front hallway like a ghost.'

My luggage was a haunting image of my former self. I didn't even have time to unpack and prepare myself for what awaited. Without warning, my comfortable and ordinary life changed when a stranger ran a red light.

That night, I kept thinking about everything Mom and Tammy had told me. *This is really bad.* I closed my eyes.

The next day, I woke up, ready to ask more questions. I had forgotten that it was the weekend, and that I would spend this time at home with my family. Both Mom and

Dad picked me up. This time, I kept quiet about the ramp. It was still there.

Mom handed me a cup of coffee and sat with me at the kitchen table. Dad sat down next to me, too. I asked, 'Is it okay if we talk some more?'

'Yes,' Dad said. 'The doctor said we should wait for you to start asking questions before talking to you about it. Whatever you need to know, Julie. We'll try to answer as best we can.'

'Thanks.' I took a sip of my coffee, then asked, 'So what else happened that first night after Dr Shea left?'

'We tried to sleep in the waiting room. No one wanted to go home and leave you by yourself. The next morning your dad finally got a copy of the accident report.'

'Dad, what did it say? What happened?' *Who ran into me? I need to know.*

'A teenage boy in a burgundy Oldsmobile ran a red light.'

'And that's all we know?'

'That's basically everything in the report,' Dad said. 'I talked to the police later, and they said he was running late for a community college class.'

That's unbelievable. This accident didn't have to happen!
'Dad, then what?' I managed to ask.

'Marion Denk, our neighbor, dropped by the hospital to see how you were doing. I took her into your room, and Dr Shea came in with an entourage of interns. He went to your bed and shouted, "Julie! Wake up! Can you hear me?" Of course you didn't do anything. Then he said, "Julie, stick out your tongue." He told the interns that the most difficult thing you could do is to stick out your tongue on command. He asked them to wait in the hall while he spoke with me.'

'What did he say?' I shifted positions in my chair.

64

'He looked real serious. I asked, "How's my daughter?" He asked me if I understood how injured you were. I nodded. I knew. You were on life support. He looked me straight in the eye and said, "It doesn't look good. I don't know if your daughter will ever wake up. If she does, she'll probably need long-term care for the rest of her life."' Dad moved his chair closer to mine. 'I told him, "I hear what you're saying, Doctor, but I know that Julie still has life in her. If God wants her to die, then he'll take her home. I will not pull the plugs! I have faith that my daughter will be okay. I don't know exactly what shape 'okay' will be, but we'll take it."'

Even the doctor knew how bad it was.

'Julie,' my dad said in his emphatic tone, 'I just want you to know something. Your mom and I never considered pulling those plugs. We knew that you would wake up and breathe on your own.'

'But how could you know that?' It was difficult to hear that pulling plugs was a distinct possibility.

'I don't know. But I just knew.' *If you only knew where I actually was, Dad. If you only knew.* But I wasn't ready to share my experience with him. Not yet.

I sipped my coffee and continued to ask more questions. 'So what happened?'

'Marion Denk started sobbing. I forgot that she was still in the room. I went to your side and kept shouting, "Wake up, Julie! Stick out your tongue! Stick out your tongue!"'

'Dad, you really thought I was going to die?' My voice was shaky. This was a difficult question for me to ask my dad.

'You should know something. Later that afternoon, the priest from our church walked into the ICU waiting room to pray with us and share words of comfort. Everyone knew the real reason he was there. We all walked together to your room, and he performed the last rites.'

I'm not surprised. After all, I was in heaven.

'Julie, I want you to know that our prayers and faith got us through this.'

God's getting me through this too, Dad.

Feeling the need to comfort my parents, I said, 'I love you. Thanks for everything you've done. But, you know something? I'm a child of God. He'll take care of everything. I know.' *I was in the light. I was in heaven!*

Dad smiled and said, 'We know that.'

'If it's not too hard on you, I'd like to hear more. What else did I miss when I was in the coma?' I needed the missing sequence to properly connect the muddled pieces.

'Dr Shea checked on you every day. He explained that after forty-eight hours in a coma with no change in neurological function, it would be more difficult for you to wake up. If you did wake up, you wouldn't be able to take care of yourself. He encouraged us to do things that would be familiar to you. Brett made cassette tapes with your favorite music, and he even put the headphones on you.'

I laughed. 'That must have looked funny. So when did the machines come off?'

'You got the feeding tube put in around the seventh day, and by the tenth day you were weaned from the ventilator and breathed on your own. On the eleventh day, a miracle happened.'

'A real miracle,' Mom interjected. 'That day, when Dr Shea shouted, "Stick out your tongue," you did! We couldn't believe it. Everyone cheered and thanked God. Dr Shea practically cried. All he could say was, "This is amazing. What a great thing!" It was definitely one of the best days of our lives.'

I can't believe that sticking out my tongue is such a big deal. But I think I understand. When my big toe moved, I felt the significance.

Dad jumped in, 'Julie, when you stuck out your tongue, that showed us that our prayers and the prayers of others were being answered. I couldn't believe how many people were praying for you, even strangers.'

'So, what happened after I stuck out my tongue?'

'Days passed, and even though you stayed in a coma, nobody gave up. Eventually, they moved you out of ICU and onto a regular floor. Since you kept getting pneumonia, the nurses strapped you in a cardiac chair several hours a day to keep you upright.'

So even then I was strapped in.

Mom continued, 'We all just settled into a daily routine. We'd come to the hospital each morning at 8:30 or 9:00, and stay until 10:00 at night. Each morning in the parking lot, I'd look up at your window on the second floor and just picture that one day you'd be standing there, waiting and waving.'

I wanted to hear more, but I needed help getting to the bathroom. Mom wheeled me and helped lift me onto the toilet. 'I need to lie down for awhile.'

I slept for a few hours and woke up hungry. Mom heated up some mashed potatoes in the microwave. I loved mashed potatoes. I asked her for more details: I wanted to continue our conversation. 'How long was I at Loyola?'

'Seventeen days,' Mom answered.

'When and how did I go to the rehabilitation hospital?'

'Your dad worked very hard to arrange that one. No one thought that you'd wake up. They wanted you to go to a nursing home. Loyola couldn't do anything else to take care of you medically. You were unresponsive.'

Dad came into the kitchen. 'Are you talking about the rehabilitation hospital?'

'Yes. Julie was asking how she ended up there.' Mom handed him a plate of mashed potatoes to put on the table.

'All of your charts kept saying unresponsive, but we didn't lose hope,' Dad said. 'We knew you were lost inside somewhere. One night you put your arm around Jill. We couldn't believe it. She sat so still, afraid to move. A nurse ran in and pulled you away from her, worried about all the excitement. They explained it away as an "involuntary movement," but we all knew that you were reaching out.'

Poor Jill. That must have been difficult for her. She is one of my closest friends, and her father died from a brain aneurism shortly before my accident.

Mom jumped into the conversation. 'The morning after you hugged Jill, some people came to your room to take you to a nursing home. We had no idea they were coming for you. Your dad refused to let them take you. He said that he'd call the insurance company and handle this himself.'

'Yeah,' Dad said. 'I was furious that someone was trying to take you away. People were just giving up. That was killing me. I finally got the supervisor on the phone and demanded, "Give my daughter a chance. She needs rehabilitation therapy. She's going to wake up." The guy on the phone said that the files showed you were unresponsive. I told him, "She stuck out her tongue. She hugged her friend. She's responsive. Just give her a chance!"'

'That's your father. He refused to take "no" for an answer. It was his persistence and the support of Dr Shea that changed the minds of that insurance company,' Mom said, and squeezed Dad's arm.

'But I gotta tell ya,' Dad said with a frown. 'It's been the hardest thing as parents for us to leave you at the rehabilitation hospital. But don't get me wrong: we were happy to have you there instead of the nursing home.'

Mom put down the dishtowel and said, 'When we first got a tour of the place, your dad and I went back to the car and cried. But you know, Julie, it's the best place for you to be. Day one they had you up and doing physical therapy six days a week. You looked like a limp rag doll, even when we yelled for you to wake up.'

Dad grinned. 'And look at you now. You're awake and you're doin' great.'

That night, when the nurse changed my diaper and strapped me in bed, I didn't feel alone. I fell asleep, eager to participate in the sessions the next day. As a professional, I always set goals and expectations for myself and worked hard to achieve them. I knew that 'my body would heal'. Although I didn't know what that ultimately meant, I wanted to work my hardest to reach my fullest potential. In physical therapy, I made great strides since the room stopped spinning. I was able to walk with assistance while wearing my purple brace. One evening, I even walked to the end of my hallway. Almost ten feet. Tammy and her husband, John, were visiting me that night. John followed me with the wheelchair, just in case I needed to collapse into it. Other patients in their wheelchairs cheered me on. Getting to know some of the other patients was a highlight during my stay. After breakfast each morning, Fran, a lovely older woman who suffered a stroke, would come to my room. Over a cup of coffee, we would talk. I enjoyed my conversations about work with Joe, a fellow businessman and brain injury survivor. We enjoyed referring to sales volume, income and other business terms. With Steve, a high school student, I discussed my fears about life outside and what was going to happen 'out there.' Marianjoy became a community, a neighborhood.

Toward the end of my stay at the rehabilitation hospital, I shared a room with a young mother who was in a coma. Her husband and pre-school-age son came each day to visit. One afternoon, the child put his chin on the footboard of my bed and curiously peered at me.

'Hi,' I whispered, sensing he had something to tell me.

'Hi,' the young boy said, somewhat startled. 'You're not asleep.'

'No, I'm awake,' I smiled at him.

'My mommy's sleeping.' He edged closer and tugged at my covers.

'Yes, your mommy's sleeping. A few weeks ago, I was sleeping, too.'

'You were?'

'Yes.'

'Did it hurt?'

'No. I didn't feel any pain while I was sleeping, and your mommy doesn't feel any pain either.' The young boy smiled and ran back to his dad, who was standing by the door. His dad whispered, 'Thank you' to me.

Later that day, I shared that experience with my mother and said, 'One day I want to be a voice for people who cannot speak.' I knew that would be the ultimate purpose of my recovery – the reason for the gift. But first, I had to heal.

CHAPTER EIGHT

MIXED EMOTIONS:
PREPARING TO GO HOME

Along with the milestones, I had setbacks. Occupational therapy was particularly difficult. My left arm didn't progress as quickly as my left leg. Sheila asked me to flip quarters from one side to the next with my left hand. I looked at the coin. *This takes such ridiculous effort.* Thirty minutes later, I flipped one. Tammy cheered as if I were a recipient of a Nobel Prize. I thought, *Look what my life has come to – excitement over flipping a coin!*

One person did not encourage me. She said, 'You do realize that you'll probably never be able to live on your own, drive or work again. Let's just be realistic about your expectations of recovery from this type of injury.'

How dare someone tell me what I will not be able to do? Like everyone else, people with brain injuries have feelings. Even though the body may be disabled, the heart is able. This person automatically presumed that since I suffered such a severe brain stem injury I should be unable to function at higher levels. Presumption promotes prejudice.

Once a week, the traumatic brain injury survivors were all wheeled into a common area for special programs and presentations. I looked around the room. We were all in diapers. Many of us had feeding tubes and remnant patches of baldness from neurosurgery. At that moment, I realized that brain injury does not discriminate against age, race or gender. Each of us was different, yet we were all the same. We were survivors, bonded together as family to face a new kind of life. Looking around the room, I felt a surge of unbridled compassion for each person. I wondered if any of them had also visited heaven. My experience in the light only confirmed what I had always known before. We all come from the same place, and we are going back to the same place. So why is the world so far apart now? Why should segregation or prejudice have any place in our lives?

After lunch each day, I took a nap. Either my parents or one of my friends were there when I woke up. On one of her many visits, Jill sat by my side.

'Dad told me about the day I hugged you. What happened?'

'You were just staring straight ahead like a zombie in your cardiac chair. I knelt next to you and asked, "How are you?" I saw a tear stream down your cheek, so I whispered, "Julie, it's okay to cry. It's okay to feel sad about everything." You looked trapped, unable to express everything that was inside of you. I hugged you, and then you put your arm around me.'

I still feel trapped. I whispered, 'Will you please stay and hold my hand until I fall asleep?' *I still feel scared and alone*.

Sue was also there for me many times. While my parents took a class to learn how to care for me at home, Sue stayed with me. Sometimes her husband Mike would come with her. I will never forget the few days when Sue took her children to visit her parents in New York.

'Are you sure you don't mind my not being here, Julie?' she asked.

Even though I would miss her visits, I said, 'Go. I'll be

fine.' I was surprised yet appreciative that Mike continued to visit me while she was away. He was there when my ex-husband walked into my room. Mike excused himself to the hallway.

'Can I come in?' my ex-husband asked. (Out of respect, I would like not to use his real name, but rather call him Bill.)

'Sure,' I said. He watched in shock as I dragged my leg over so I could sit on the side of the bed.

'You're paralyzed! I'm so sorry. I can't believe this happened to you.' I sensed his genuine sorrow and concern. Although I was surprised by his visit, I knew in my heart that he would show up some day. How could he not? We were married for five years, and we had dated seven years prior to that. Yes, we were legally apart, but emotionally, Bill would always be a special part of my life.

'Yes. It happened. And it's changed my life forever.'

'I've been worried about you.' He stood in front of me. 'You know that Loyola called me first after your accident?'

'I heard. Thanks for giving them my parents' phone number.' I was glad that the divorce was not a bitter one. I would always be grateful that Bill gave the information to Loyola for the chaplain to contact my parents.

Mike came back in the room. 'Sorry to interrupt, but usually we take Julie outside about this time.' Mike helped me into the wheelchair. Bill walked with us to the outdoor patio. We talked for awhile. After their class ended, my parents joined us outside and didn't appear shocked to see Bill. They even thanked him in person for giving their phone number to the hospital. Everyone exchanged pleasantries, and a few minutes later, my ex-husband left.

Mom looked over at me and asked, 'How do you feel?' I knew she was inquiring about seeing Bill for the first time in over a year.

'I'm fine.' As I watched Bill leave, I knew that an important chapter of my life had ended. It wasn't a happily-ever-after ending, but I felt at peace and full of faith that God would lead the way.

Just days before my release, an embarrassing moment happened. I got my period for the first time since before the accident. Of course, the only male nurse was on duty that morning. Strong and Nordic-looking, this nurse wheeled me into the bathroom so I could work on my 'potty training'. Sitting on the toilet, I realized immediately that my period had returned. I pushed the call button.

'Is everything okay?' He stood outside the bathroom door and asked.

'Well, not exactly. I just got my period.' How humiliating. I was sitting on the toilet having this unbelievable conversation.

'No way,' he responded in disbelief, 'Female patients just coming out of comas don't get their period!'

'Trust me, I did,' I blushed. 'Can you please get a sanitary pad for me?' *This goes beyond embarrassment. I can't believe that I have to deal with a period while I'm paralyzed. Diapers, cramps, and sanitary pads?*

'Since nobody gets their period on this floor, we don't have any pads around here. I'm sorry.' I could tell he was embarrassed. What male wouldn't be embarrassed to have this discussion with a woman?

'Well, do you think you can find one for me?' With my right arm, I balanced myself on the toilet so I wouldn't tip over.

'Of course. I'll be right back.' I heard his footsteps quickly leave my room.

Moments later, a female nurse knocked on the bathroom door. I was still holding onto the rail, trying to remain seated on the toilet.

'Julie,' she exclaimed, 'your recovery is absolutely spectacular. This just doesn't happen.'

'I need a pad, please.' At this point, I was desperate.

'Of course, hon. I'll get a pad from my purse for you right away.'

I would later learn from my neurosurgeon that getting a period so quickly after such a severe brain stem injury was very unusual. He explained that typically in an injury such as mine, the hypothalamus, the body's regulator for hormones, gets so discombobulated that a female usually will not get her period for at least a year post-coma. *Lucky me!* It was obvious to everyone that my body was starting to heal. I just wasn't fully prepared for the consequences.

A few days before officially being discharged, the nurses presented me with a 'Most Improved Patient' award. It was the first time that they had ever given an award like that to anyone. *Most improved? I still have such a long way to go.*

On the day of my release, I felt a combination of emotions. I was excited and afraid. When my primary nurse told me that I would go home that day, I didn't know what to say or how to feel. 'I can't leave!' *What I mean to say is that I can't envision leaving a place where I have become so comfortable. It's hard to explain.*

My primary nurse had become my surrogate mom throughout my whole stay. She was small, strong, and feisty, just like my mother. 'I can't leave. My parents don't know how to take care of a disabled person.'

Yet my parents *were* ready, and they knew how to care for me in my disabled state. They had been taking classes. I was the one who wasn't ready. I felt different. *I just want to be like everyone else. But I feel so different. I don't want anyone to feel sorry for me.*

Two and a half months after my accident, I became one

of the 80,000 traumatic brain injury survivors who leave the hospital each year with a disability. The nurse and my parents wheeled me outside into the parking lot. I was overcome with fear. *What is my life going to be like? I don't know what it's like to live as a disabled person. I'm only twenty-nine! Divorced and now disabled. Do I have to start over again?*

Chapter Nine

Retying the Apron Strings: Life as an Adult Child

With 'apron strings' reattached, I returned to my childhood home in Downer's Grove. As Dad wheeled me up that frustrating ramp, I bit my lip and tears gathered. *So here I am, back at my parents' home. I can't even walk up the steps I used to run up.* I looked at the backyard where I used to spend hours as a child, running, skipping, and jumping rope.

Dad pushed the wheelchair into the house.

'Julie, we've got your old room all ready for you,' Mom said. 'We even moved your double bed out from storage from your apartment.' I had not slept in this room since I left home at age twenty-one to marry Bill.

'I can get out now and walk,' I said in my most defiant voice.

'Okay,' Dad said, as he steadied me onto my feet. He helped me walk through the living room into my bedroom. I glanced around. Reality hit. *I'm not here for quick visits anymore. I'm here to live. This is hard to believe.*

'Here's a brass bell by your bed if you need us in the night,' Mom said, placing a suitcase on the bed. 'Also, Dad put some bars by the toilet and hooked up a hand-held shower for you, too.'

This is my life. I can't shower without help. A childhood bell is next to my adult bed. 'Thanks,' I said, looking around.

'I'm sorry you guys had to lose an extra TV room.'

'Don't even think about that for a second,' Dad said.

That night, as I lay in my room, I could almost hear echoes from my childhood – the late night giggles with Tammy, the pillow fights, and the soft scolds from Mom and Dad, saying, 'Go to sleep, girls.' *God, I'm back where I started. I haven't even lived my life yet. I'm twenty-nine and living at home like a child. Do I really have to go through all this again?*

Then I did something that I should have done before. I surrendered my whole recovery to God. It was evident that I was still dependent on having a wheelchair in close proximity. I wanted to believe that I would no longer need it. However, I was at last ready to accept a limitation to my healing process. In my heart, I prayed, *God, if this is the extent of my recovery, thank you. You have already brought me further along than anyone could ever imagine. Please help me accept that I might need a wheelchair for the rest of my life if that is part of the plan. Please help me adjust to living at home with my parents. Please just stay by my side and help me through each day.*

The next day, my new routine began. I woke up at six o'clock. Mom helped me to the bathroom, got me dressed, then walked with me into the kitchen for breakfast. Pouring a cup of coffee, she said, 'You start your outpatient rehabilitation today. It's in St Charles. Not far away. You'll go there three times a week.' I nodded, while carefully holding a glass of orange juice. Mom continued, 'I'll drive you there and back today, but starting tomorrow, a taxi will pick you up. I took off from work today.' *And so it continues…*

I liked my physical therapist, Sally. As she stretched each leg, Sally asked, 'What are your personal goals for these sessions?'

'If it's at all possible, I want to get out of the wheelchair forever.' She bent my left leg in circular motions. 'And I want to live on my own and get back to work. But if I remain in the wheelchair, I just want to be able to function as best as my body can.'

'Okay. We'll get you up and walking as much as possible. Looks like your left arm needs more movement.' Sally was right. My left shoulder was frozen. Caring for myself was challenging. To stimulate movement in my shoulder, I was given huge cortisone shots. I couldn't feel a thing when a huge needle pierced my skin.

Three days a week, the taxi picked me up at my parents' house. It was usually the same driver. Mom wheeled me down the ramp and helped me into the taxi while the driver stored my wheelchair in the trunk. This was a very defining time for me. Prior to my sessions with Sally, I came to terms with the real possibility of staying in a wheelchair. *God, if I'm in this wheelchair forever, please help me accept that. If not, please help me get out and find what I'm supposed to do for you.*

At each session, Sally kept stretching my legs and walking by my side in the hallway, ready to catch me if I tripped. We were both pleased and surprised with my progress. She determined that I was ready to start walking outside on the sidewalk. Sally said, 'I think you're ready for the next step.'

I closed my eyes in the backseat of the taxi. It had been an exhausting day. The taxi driver interrupted: 'What kinds of food do you like?'

'What?' I opened my eyes, surprised by his question.

'Do you like to eat different kinds of food?'

'Sure. I like everything.'

'Do you go out to restaurants?'

'Sometimes on weekends.' *Why is he asking me these strange questions?*

'Would you like to go to a restaurant with me?'

'Thanks, but I'm just not ready for that.' I shook my head and closed my eyes. I didn't have the energy yet to deal with dating.

Nothing more was ever said. The next morning, I was happy that a different driver showed up at the house.

The discipline of my training for a biathlon prior to the accident helped me prepare for the next stage of my recovery. I stayed focused on my goals and continued to push myself to achieve them. Just as I trained for running, I trained for walking. Sally and I walked a little faster and a little farther during each session. I thrived on pushing myself to my physical limit. Athletes are comfortable with that goal. My gait, however, was not like that of the models walking the runways of New York during Fashion Week. With each step, I had to exert an exorbitant amount of energy to concentrate on pulling my left leg forward. I still had a brace attached to it, but I was walking. Praise God! I was walking!

Weeks later, I refused to take my wheelchair to outpatient rehabilitation anymore. The possibility of living on my own again and going back to work inched closer to a tangible edge of reality.

One morning at breakfast, I told my parents, 'Please get rid of the wheelchair ramp. I don't need it anymore.'

Remembering our previous conversation about the ramp on Father's Day, Dad understood his youngest daughter's intentions. When I returned from outpatient rehabilitation that day, the ramp was gone. The removal of the ramp was like the tearing down of the Berlin Wall and the fall of the walls of Jericho. My quest for independence symbolically began.

Although I felt resilient at home, I still felt vulnerable whenever I was in public. One evening, Jill and I went to dinner at a local restaurant. When we walked in, I had to take very slow and deliberate steps. Step right. Pull left.

Sitting down, I whispered, 'Jill, everyone is staring at me.'

Jill reassured me, 'Julie, it's okay. No one's staring.'

'But I never wanted to become a spectacle.' I couldn't stop my tears.

Jill nodded her head, acknowledging my feelings as I sat in silence. *I've been robbed of my self-confidence.*

'You'll be okay, Julie. Just give it time. You've been through a lot.' Her friendship has been a true support during my greatest time of need.

My parents noticed my giant steps toward physical recovery and independence. One evening after therapy, I was not yet home from my sessions. The new cab driver got lost on the way back to the house. I did what was natural for my old self. I was able to lead. I helped him find the way. When I arrived home, Mom was on the phone with the cab company, looking very worried. 'Why were you so concerned?' I asked. 'I can manage these things on my own.' That night a little self-confidence was injected into my deflated image.

Just a month after I returned home, a telephone call opened a fast track for my independence. Dad seemed eager to say something to me during dinner. He put his elbows on the table and asked in his matter-of-fact tone, 'Julie, how do you feel about driving?'

Caught off guard, I thought to myself, *Drive again? How scary. But I need to be able to drive to have my independence.*

'I'd like to drive. Why?' I looked over at Dad, uncertain what had prompted his question.

'I got a phone call today from your old rehab hospital. They asked if you'd be interested in driving again.'

'What did you say?' I felt my food dance in my stomach.

'I asked what we needed to do.'

'Well, what do we need to do?' I pushed my plate toward the center of the table and leaned forward.

'I guess you're interested then, right?' He smiled his big grin.

My smile answered any doubt Dad might have had.

'You'll need to take a special two-and-a-half-hour test to show you're mentally and physically able to drive again. You can take it at the rehab facility. We'll call them when you're ready.'

'Okay. What's next?' *I can't believe I'm going to drive again! Driving almost killed me. Do I really want to do this?*

'Great! Let's go for it! We'll go to the same parking lot where you first learned.'

We returned to my teenage driving spot so I could relearn how to drive. Dad was a great coach. 'Get behind the wheel,' he said, ready to climb into the passenger side.

Wrapping the knuckles of my right hand around the steering wheel, I felt nervous. I had not driven since 10 May. *I can do this. Just remember what to do.* With no memories of the accident, I had no flashbacks to haunt me. The only accident I remembered was at age seventeen. I was backing the Buick out of the garage and ran into a huge lilac bush in the driveway. It left a big dent in the car and a broken bush on the ground. Luckily, I worked at an outdoor nursery, so I could replace the lilac, but I couldn't restore the huge dent. I knew my dad would be upset at me. I was upset at myself. When I got to work, I sat on a bench and cried. Bill, my ex-husband, was my co-worker at that time. He consoled me, assuring me that everything would be okay. That night, I explained to my dad why the lilac bush was broken and showed him the big dent in the car. Dad didn't yell. He only asked if I had been hurt. Then, throughout the evening, I heard the sound of metal pounding as Dad worked for hours to remove the dent.

Dad leaned over to help buckle my seatbelt and asked, 'Are you ready for this?'

I nodded and gripped the steering wheel even more tightly with my right hand.

'Do you remember what to do next?' His blue eyes looked at me, trying to assess what I could do. I can imagine how nervous he must have felt, teaching his brain-injured daughter who could only use her right side how to drive again. But Dad remained calm and determined to help.

Loosening my grip on the steering wheel, I used my right hand to turn on the ignition, then shifted the gear into drive. I was grateful for the ability to use my right foot for pressing the brake and accelerator pedals.

'You're doing great. It's all coming back to you.' Dad said. Behind the wheel, I felt able but so afraid. With each maneuver that I was able to accomplish, I gained more confidence. The repetition reminded my brain what I already knew how to do. I could drive! I was on the road to independence.

After many weekend practice sessions, I felt ready for the driving exam. Dad called and made arrangements. On 9 September 1993, almost four months to the day after my accident, I was ready to take my test. Dad dropped me off in front of the rehabilitation hospital and parked the car. Waiting outside, I recalled a vivid memory – sitting in the garden patio in my wheelchair. Each afternoon and evening, someone would wheel me outside for fresh air. I would watch the cars drive by and think, *Look at how my life has stopped. Their lives just go on.*

I never wanted something so badly as to pass this test. I needed a reinstated license to be able to drive to my job and provide for myself. The woman assigned to give me the actual driving test walked toward me. 'Are you Julie?'

'Yes,' I said, trying to stand a little taller and straighter.

'I bet you're ready to get this over with, aren't you?' she asked with a smile.

'Yes,' I said. She directed me to a specially equipped car with steering wheels and brakes on both the driver's and passenger's side. *What a stressful job to have. I can't imagine how unsafe it must feel to give a driving test to people who have been seriously injured.* I was determined to impress her with my ability and agility, even though I could only move my right side.

She asked me to turn right out of the parking lot and onto Roosevelt Road, a four lane street. I carefully steered and thanked God she didn't have me turn left. It felt strange, yet familiar to drive with other cars again. Dad and I had only practiced in the parking lot, not the street. Everything was going just fine until the woman felt that I was not stopping soon enough when the car in front of me braked. She slammed on the brakes on the passenger's side. The jolt of the stop shocked me. I burst into tears and begged, 'Please don't flunk me. Please. I have to pass this test.'

'Julie, you're doing great,' the woman reassured me. 'I just thought we were a little close, that's all, but it is quite evident that you know how to drive.' As we pulled back into the parking lot, I was shaking. She led me into the building so I could take the written exam. That day, I learned that I passed the tests, and my Illinois driver's license would be reinstated within a few weeks. I hugged my mom and dad who were waiting for me. I knew that I would be an extremely careful driver. I never wanted anyone to be hurt from what I did behind the wheel.

Although I regained freedom to drive again, I felt that the apron strings were turning into a noose around my neck at home. I became more aggravated as my parents unintentionally interfered with my quest for independence. Parents are inherently protective. With a disabled child, parents sometimes become over-protective.

One afternoon, I carefully and slowly walked down the basement steps, placing two feet on each step, to get a lemonade soda from the refrigerator for my mom. I wanted to surprise her. I no longer even needed to wear my purple leg brace. When I walked back up the stairs, my dad's tall frame loomed large under the basement door.

'Be careful!' he chided. 'You're not supposed to walk down the stairs without help.'

I wanted to scream, *Dad, I'm not a kid! I'm a careful adult! Stop hovering over me. Please!* All I could say was, 'I'm sorry.'

Later that same day, Mom said, 'Julie, you seem to be getting around much better. Why don't you help me vacuum the house?' It was like a flashback from childhood: assigned weekend chores.

Vacuum the house? If I can vacuum your house then I can vacuum a home of my own. I have to move out of here. I appreciate everything you guys have done for me, but I need to breathe. All I could say was, 'Okay, Mom, I'll vacuum.'

CHAPTER TEN

FALLING IN LOVE:
A SENSE OF NORMALCY

'What would you do if your sink had a leak?' my speech therapist in outpatient rehabilitation asked.

'Call a plumber,' I answered.

'How would you find a plumber?'

'Look one up in the phone book,' I said with a sarcastic tone. *Why is she asking me these questions?*

'So you want to live on your own?' She raised her eyebrows and looked me in the eyes to assess my level of intent.

'Yes.' My answer was emphatic. A serious commitment to this dream.

'Then I have a graduation assignment for you. Find an apartment that's handicap accessible.'

Up for the challenge, I asked for a phone book and looked up a listing for an apartment finder. I dialed the number.

'Hello, this is George,' a voice answered on the other end.

'Hi, George,' I said, trying to articulate clearly in front of my therapist. 'My name is Julie Papievis, and I am looking for a handicap accessible apartment.' Since my accident, my voice has changed because of vocal cord damage. It is somewhat lower and softer now. Friends tease me, saying that I sound quite 'sultry.'

'Well, I can help you,' he said.

We spoke for a long time, discussing apartment locations and amenities. He had no idea that I suffered from a brain stem injury, and I did not tell him. I told him that I didn't plan to move into an apartment until December. He said that he would be glad to show some apartments to me at my convenience. Over the next few weeks, we spoke numerous times. One day, George asked me out under the pretext of looking at a possible apartment.

'Julie, why don't we get together this weekend, so I can show you a great place?'

'I'm sorry, I have to attend a benefit.' I held onto the phone with my right hand.

'What's the benefit for?' He sounded curious.

'It's actually for me.' I looked at the ground. How humbling it was to think about the fund-raiser that my parents' neighbors, Bill and Marion Denk, along with Tammy, had planned for me on 17 September 1993. The healthcare bills were piling up, and insurance companies had not yet settled everything.

'Where's it being held?'

'At the Willowbrook Holiday Inn.'

On the day of the benefit, I spent a long time to get ready for the event. Carmen, one of the best makeup artists who worked for me when I was an account executive with a major cosmetics firm, did my makeup. We both realized the poignancy of that moment as she applied the blush on my high cheekbones. It was difficult for both of us. We both held back our tears, not wanting to upset the other and of course not wanting the makeup to smear. Debbi, a friend I grew up with, did my hair. Mom helped me put on the black vested pantsuit with flared legs that Tammy and I bought at Ann Taylor. I wore a crisp white blouse underneath. I chose to wear flats beneath the flared pant legs that hid my purple leg brace. Balancing and walking in high heels was not yet an option for me.

On the night of the benefit, I was surrounded by over 200 people from different parts of my life who were there to help me financially and to tell me how happy they were that I had survived. While sitting at the registration and raffle ticket table, I greeted each guest and thanked everyone for coming. Like Jimmy Stewart in *It's a Wonderful Life*, I was overwhelmed by the number of people who showed up to help me in my time of need. I couldn't believe that my grade school superintendent was there. He saw me at the table and said, 'I read about your accident in the paper, and when I heard there was going to be a benefit, I just had to come. I couldn't believe that one of my students suffered such a horrific injury. I had to come and offer support to you and your family.'

My brother Brett stayed close by my side. His friend had donated his services to be a DJ for the benefit so that there would be music and dancing. Brett helped me navigate through the crowd so I could thank his friend. Brett said, 'Julie, you need to dance.' He let me step onto his feet, so I could 'dance.' As a child, I would step onto Dad's feet, too, so he could twirl me around and dance. Although I smiled at the guests, I still felt disconnected, like I was just an observer. An invisible spectator.

'Brett, I feel like I'm at my own wake.' I didn't mean to say those words. They just slipped out. It was the only description in my own mind that explained my feelings that evening. It was a surreal experience.

'That's not even funny,' he said with a serious look. I didn't want to upset Brett. How could I explain to him that being alive was a lot more difficult than being dead? I had to ride on his feet so I could dance. When would I be able to share my experience in heaven with someone? It was the loneliest feeling not to be able to share something so significant with those I loved. However, I still wasn't ready. So I did what felt the most natural thing to do at that moment. I laughed and said, 'Oh, Brett, don't take it so seriously.'

After the dance with my brother, I looked around and saw my cousin Ray speaking to a tall, handsome man. Immediately, I knew who that person was, and I approached him.

My cousin said, 'Julie, you have to meet a friend of mine.'

Before Ray could finish his sentence, the handsome stranger extended his hand and said, 'Hi, Julie. I'm George, the apartment finder.'

As I shook his hand, I smiled and said, 'Yes, yes, I figured that's who you were.' His handshake was strong, and his words were gentle. I felt an immediate attraction to this man whom I only knew through the phone.

'Hey, did you know that George helped me find my new apartment?' Ray asked. But I barely heard what he was saying. I couldn't believe George had actually come to the benefit. What guts! I admired that.

We walked to the hotel lobby to talk. The music started playing again, and it was difficult to raise my voice. I felt like we had already developed a friendship over the phone, and I wanted to explain my accident to him. We found some chairs, and I started talking.

'I'd like for you to understand what happened to me. I was in a car accident in May, and I'm recovering from a severe brain stem injury.' I shared my story with him, and he listened. I sensed who he was and felt safe.

The next day he called. 'How about dinner this weekend?'

'How about a wedding?' I asked.

'What?' He sounded confused.

'My co-worker's getting married on Saturday. Do you want to go?' I explained.

'Sure. Should I pick you up at your place?'

'It's not my place. But yeah, pick me up at my parents' house.'

When Saturday came, I felt like a high school girl again, getting ready for 'date night' at my parents' home. Waiting for the doorbell to ring. Adjusting my hair one last time in front of the mirror. Applying one more layer of lipstick.

Dad opened the front door. 'I'm Jerry Papievis. You must be George. Come on in.'

George stepped in the foyer. 'Julie,' Dad called, 'George is here.'

'Thanks, Dad. I know.' *Please don't embarrass me. I'm not a teenager anymore.*

Before walking out the door, George turned to my dad and said, 'I'll take good care of her.' *What a gentleman.*

After the wedding, we walked to the car. George held my hand. Chemistry was there. He gently leaned over and kissed me. I felt feminine and attractive. But most of all, I felt so normal.

Falling in love with George achieved something beyond what any other outpatient therapy could accomplish. Once again, I became a young woman with the same hopes and dreams of a 'happily ever after' fairytale. I was Cinderella, kissed by a Prince Charming. I was in love.

CHAPTER ELEVEN

'YOU'RE MY DEAD PATIENT': MEETING DR SHEA

'You're supposed to be dead. You're my dead patient.' A silver-haired doctor walked into the examination room holding a heavy medical chart.

'Hi, I'm Julie.' I didn't know how to respond to this unexpected comment by my neurosurgeon.

'And I'm Dr Shea. I can't believe that you are sitting here in front of me, walking, talking and living.' He acknowledged my parents with a handshake.

'She can even drive now, too,' Dad added.

'Julie, you're amazing. What an incredible recovery.' He put a six-inch file on the examination table and brushed back his hair.

'Why do you say that?' I wanted to hear it straight from the doctor.

'I thought at best you would be severely disabled. I never expected a recovery, much less a good recovery after such a severe brain stem injury and after rating a three on the Glasgow Coma Scale.'

'What is that?'

'The Glasgow Coma Scale?' Dr Shea looked at me to make sure I wanted to know the medical details.

'Yeah.' My inquisitive nature was apparent to this doctor, and he proceeded to explain. No matter how difficult it would be to hear the details, I wanted to know the facts.

'It's a standardized way of assessing the likelihood of someone waking up from a coma. You were completely unresponsive and scored the lowest possible number.'

'That's the first test I ever failed.'

Dr Shea smiled. 'Actually you passed it. Only 4 percent survive when they get that score with the brain stem injury. And those that do typically don't function independently.'

'Oh.' I took a breath. I wanted more details about my injury. 'What exactly happened to me?'

'In medical terms?' His eyebrows rose.

'Yes,' I nodded.

'This happened.' He lifted the heavy medical chart. 'In a nutshell, you suffered what is known as severe diffuse axonal injury in the brain stem. We tend to live in our brain stem since it controls breathing, and regulates heartbeats, muscle movement, blood pressure and body temperature. The brain stem is like a little candle inside the head. If something blows it out, life ends.'

'Did my candle blow out?' I hesitated to ask this question, but I needed to know the truth.

'I thought it had, Julie. There's no medical reason that you should be here in my office, talking and reasoning like this. You were paralyzed, and now you're walking and driving a car.' I appreciated his direct answer. I learned a little about the function of the brain stem during my physical therapy, but I wanted to know more.

'Where is the brain stem?'

'The brain is like a ball of silly putty wrapped around a popsicle stick. Do you remember that stuff as a kid?' I nodded. Silly putty kept me entertained for hours. Rolling it flat and pressing it against newspaper print, I was amazed that the words transferred to the putty.

'The popsicle stick represents the spine. The connecting point between the spine and the brain is the brain stem. If something hits the ball of silly putty hard enough, it can turn around on the popsicle stick, slide up and down, tear and be knocked out of its original shape. The axons which carry messages from the brain stem throughout the body can be severely damaged. That's what happened to your brain. This recovery is a miracle.'

'Wow.' I didn't know what else to say. *I get it now. This recovery is a miracle.* Dr Shea began the neurological examination, checking my movement and coordination. More questions formulated in my mind. 'Dr Shea, will I continue to recover?'

'I don't know to what extent.' I appreciated the candor as he continued the examination. 'A lot about your recovery surprises me, including how thin you are. Most people tend to gain weight after being in a coma, due to the body's metabolic rate changes and inactivity.'

'I inherited my Grandpa John's genes. He was always tall and thin.'

Writing some notes in the medical chart, Dr Shea sat on the stool next to the table. He had a serious face.

'Let's talk. How are you feeling? Really feeling.'

'I'm okay. It's all a bit overwhelming, but I'm trying. It's changed *everything*.'

'I know.' He nodded his head. 'Julie, I don't want you ever to be overwhelmed by the frustration of your body not keeping up with your mind.' *He's right. My mind zooms, while my body works in deliberate motion.*

'I want you or your parents to call me if you ever need me. It's important that you keep this number and know that I am always here for you.' He handed me his home phone number.

'Why do you sound so concerned?' I didn't understand the urgent tone of his voice.

'Honestly? I'm worried. A large percentage of those very few patients that survive this severe injury end up committing suicide. They can't accept who they have become.'

The room was silent. That was a lot to hear. I spoke. 'No. I can't take the life back that God has given me. I couldn't do that to him or my parents.' The reality was that I was afraid to survive a suicide attempt, knowing the further pain it would cause my parents. The scene of my parents discovering my dead body in bed haunted me. As much as I wanted to go back into the peace of the light, I knew that in my heart I couldn't take my own life. I couldn't disappoint God.

'I hope not.' He shut my medical file and stood. 'But keep my number. Just in case.'

Before walking out of the room, he turned and asked, 'Julie, have you applied yet for Social Security disability?'

'Why would I need to do that?' I did not feel disabled. My body was healing.

'You need to do that so you can get insurance from Medicare. You have to be on Social Security disability for two years before qualifying for Medicare.' He looked at me, trying to be tender with his words.

'But I don't need Medicare. I plan to go back to work. I have insurance there.' My therapy sessions were moving forward, and financial independence was my ultimate goal. Why was he asking these questions?

'We need to talk.' Dr Shea dragged the stool next to me. The metal sound against the floor startled me. 'Julie, you have a permanent disability. No one will insure you. I don't know the specific terms of the coverage where you work now, but when you leave there one day to work elsewhere, there won't be coverage, on account of the pre-existing condition of a severe brain stem injury. Because of your situation, catching a common cold can be life-threatening to you. You will require constant medical attention. You don't have a choice. I'm sorry.' His furrowed brow expressed the depth of his sincerity.

'I don't have a choice?' The reality of the lifetime repercussions from my accident slowly surfaced. I appreciated his honesty, but this was beyond difficult to hear. His diagnosis of 'permanent disability' echoed like a gong.

'Julie, I'll always be here for your medical needs. I promise.' I knew he would keep his word and thanked God for providing such an honorable person to care for my continuous medical requirements. How grateful I am that God provided not only a physician who understood the medical complexities, but someone who understood the spiritual impact of my accident. I knew then that one day I would share my experience in heaven with Dr Shea.

For my next visit with Dr Shea, I brought a college book about the brain and its functions. I have always felt that knowledge is power, so I wanted to become empowered. I read about the brain stem and the twelve cranial nerves and the purpose of axons as messengers. Carrying the big book, I waited for Dr Shea in the examination room. I had highlighted several passages that I wanted him to clarify. Dr Shea shook his head in disbelief and chuckled, pleased by my desire to learn as much as I could about my condition and willing to take the time to explain in detail what happened to me. I was now a student and survivor of a traumatic brain injury.

CHAPTER TWELVE

DECLARING INDEPENDENCE:
READY TO LIVE ON MY OWN

By October, I was ready to take an interim step toward my independence. I knew my family wouldn't let me live on my own yet, but perhaps an option could be living with my sister. I called Tammy.

'Hi, Tam. Can I move in with you guys?' I went straight to the point in my eagerness to move out.

Ever the supportive older sister, Tammy answered, 'Of course, Julie. John and I will help bring your things over this weekend.'

Living there was a key step toward reaching my huge goal of living on my own. Tammy's place became a home base. Even though I made progress toward living on my own, I still had setbacks. I had to continue to work hard on toilet training. How embarrassing to have 'accidents' at my big sister's home. However, Tammy never made me feel self-conscious about these mishaps.

In October, I reached another important goal: I returned to work. Although I could drive, I was still too afraid. Tammy drove me to my continuing rehabilitation sessions and to and from work. Working again was difficult for me, both physically and emotionally. I wanted to work so I could feel normal. But I didn't feel normal.

Where is that person who worked all the time? The top

'Go back and be happy.' This was the message in heaven from my angels, Grandma Sue and Grandma Batten ('Gram'). This picture was taken at my parents' wedding.

Photo: Mary Ann Papievis

Growing up

Who would ever believe that I was such a tomboy? This picture was taken in my parents' backyard where I would run and play for hours as a child. I was always overflowing with energy.
Photo: Jerry Papievis

Waiting for Santa. My sister Tammy and I used to wake up very early on Christmas morning, eager to open our presents.
Photo: Jerry Papievis

Special life steps

My Christening, 1964. Grandma Sue and Grandpa John are holding me.
Photo: Jerry Papievis

My First Communion, 1972. I remember this special day and the pretty dress which my mom made for me. I was a little nervous when I read a Bible verse in front of the church.
Photo: Jerry Papievis

My College Graduation, 1984. Robert Morris College in Chicago. I graduated in the top five percent of my class and looked forward to starting my career in accounting.
Photo: Jerry Papievis

My carefree high school days

I was a typical student trying to balance the academic requirements with my busy social schedule.
Photo: Courtesy of Downer's Grove North High School.

The day my life changed: May 10, 1993

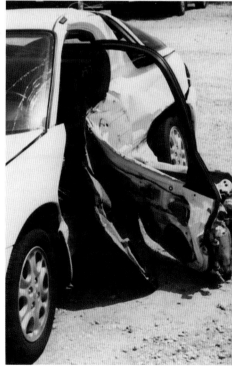

My dad had nicknamed this car 'ET' because the headlights made him think of ET's eyes. This was what was left of it after a teenager ran a red light.
Photos: Jerry Papievis

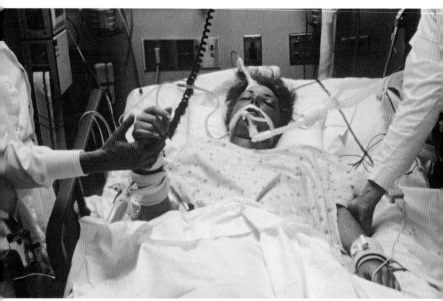

A scene from my coma. My mother thought I looked like Sleeping Beauty. This picture was taken on the night of my crash by Loyola University Medical Center in anticipation of my death.
Photo: Loyola University Medical Centre.

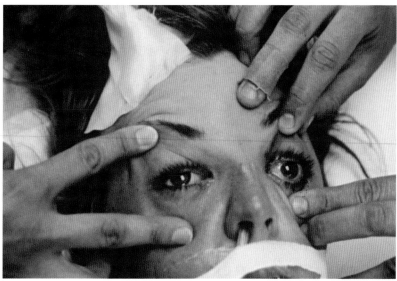

This photo shows my left pupil fully dilated due to my brain stem injury. I was not responsive. Doctors were amazed that my left side was paralysed. Usually it's the opposite side of impact.
Photo: Loyola University Medical Centre.

Starting over: Marionjoy Rehabilitation Facility

My old leg brace. I still keep it in the boot of my car as a private reminder of how far I have come. Photo: Marionjoy.

Still at a loss for words. After waking up from my month long coma, I felt overwhelmed. I was paralyzed on my left side and afraid of what the future held.

My new hairdo. My friend and hairstylist from Neiman Marcus visited me in Marianjoy and cut my hair. This new style covered up the shaved area on my head where the doctor inserted an inner cranial pressure monitor.
Photo: Nurse Zoe

NAME: _____ Julie

1. ≡ ≈
2. ‖‖‖
3. ∭
4. ∭
5. OOO
6. OOO
7. NNN
8. ◎◎
9. MMM
10. llllll

Learning to write again. Samples of my writing at Marianjoy Rehabilitation Hospital. I felt like I was back in third grade again trying my hardest to do the best that I could.

My family of 'angels'. Bottom left: My brother, Brett; my nephew Avery; my mom, who is holding my nephew Travis. Tammy's son and my Godson, Clayton; my brother-in-law John. Top left. Brett's wife, Lisa; me; my dad; Tammy.

A witness to my 'near death', Toni Rapach. She watched the teenager run the red light and felt helpless. My accident changed her life forever, too.

Vision Therapy

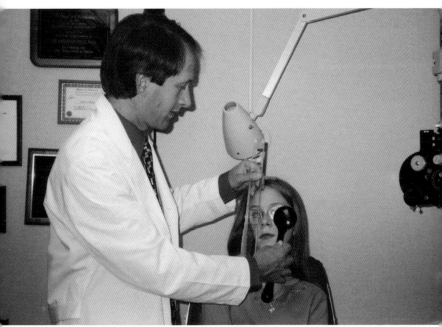

Following binocular fusion therapy, Dr Margolis checks the prism in Rachel's glasses that is designed to keep her seeing single. Photo: Dr Neil Margolis

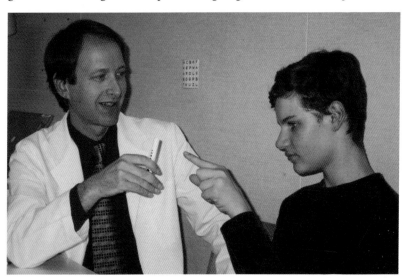

Brian Collins during his weekly vision rehabilitation session with Dr Margolis. Photo: Dr Neil Margolis.

My guiding lights

Sister Thomas Batten. She was my great aunt who always encouraged me to 'talk to Jesus.'
Photo: Mary Ann Papievis

Sister Valerie Kulbacki. For over fifteen years, she has been my counselor, trusted confidante and friend. Her wisdom helped me find my purpose.
Photo: Sister Valerie Kulbacki

Christmas lunch with my soul sisters, Sue Bentel and Jill Crosby. These special women are my best friends. Photo: Mike Bentel

Some summer fun as a counselor at the Brain Injury Association of Illinois Camp for Survivors. I enjoy our time together and the opportunity to discuss experiences, advocate for one another and share hope. Photo: Mary Coers.

A little rock and roll. Sharing a 'dance' with a fellow survivor at the Brain Injury Camp. Photo: Mary Coers.

Reaching out to the community

Visiting with the honorable Greg Ginex at a fundraiser for the Midwest Brain Injury Clubhouse. Greg is my attorney and family member who helped me with legal matters.
Photo: Kathy Dilorio

Mingling with guests at a National Brain Injury Symposium outing in Chicago. Pictured with one of my fearless leaders, Tony Romanucci, one of the partners of Romanucci & Blandin, a legal firm with whom I work.
Photo: Romanucci & Blandin

Working as a community relations advisor for Chicago law firm, Romanucci & Blandin. Pictured with Tony Romanucci.
Photo: Romanucci & Blandin

My 'medical dad', Dr John Shea, MD, Professor of Neurosurgery, Loyola University Medical Center. He calls me his 'dead patient'.
Photo: Loyola University Medical Centre

Speaking to local paramedics who were completing their trauma training at Loyola. I always welcome the opportunity to share my story with medically trained professionals.
Photo: Loyola University Medical Centre

With my friend Mary Coers, a fellow advocate and survivor.

At a brain injury clubhouse gala with my co-author, Margaret McSweeney, whose words became the voice of my heart.

I am almost there. Happily finishing my first 5K run, six years after my brain stem injury.
Photo: Jerry Papievis

I can't believe I finished! From paralysis to running a race. My recovery is truly a gift.
Photo: Jerry Papievis

The woman who made running possible, Bridget Tarrant, my physical therapist from The Rehabilitation Institute of Chicago.
Photo: Jerry Papievis

Running along Lake Michigan with the magnificent skyline of Chicago behind me. 'I have fought the good fight. I have finished the race. I have kept the faith.'

5 percent student of the college class? The hardworking accountant at McDonald's Corporation? The national cosmetic account executive with over 130 employees that reported to me? The committed administrator? What happened to that professional woman?

It was much harder to fit in with the group socially. My co-workers missed the person that I used to be, the social planner of gatherings outside of the office. I used to be part of what was known as the 'five o'clock club.' After work, I would get together with the other employees in the warehouse and socialize. Now I didn't even have enough energy to work until five. A woman at work often cried when she talked to me.

Even though I worked only three days a week, I was always exhausted. I couldn't grasp a pen and coordinate it with my fingers. I did not know how to *work* as a disabled person. I was still learning how to *live* as a disabled person.

I was grateful for my relationship with George. We continued to see each other since the fund-raiser in September. He was supportive and caring.

One day, George called me at work and said, 'Julie, I found a great place for you. It's in an apartment complex that has a great gym facility. You've got to see it.'

When I saw the place, I longed to live there on my own. But I also realized that I would need to get over my fear of driving and get a car to be truly independent. I asked my dad to go with me to a few dealerships for some test drives. My first priority was to feel safe, so I decided on an SUV, the biggest and highest car around.

At the dealership, I saw what I thought was the car of my dreams – a blue SUV. 'It looks nice,' my dad commented, checking out the features.

'Why don't you try it out for yourself?' a cheerful

salesman suggested when he saw me peeking through the windows for a look.

'Sure, okay,' I said and opened the door. I tried to climb in, but I wasn't physically able to pull myself into the car.

Not realizing that I was a survivor of a severe brain stem injury, the salesman quipped, 'Well, I guess you can't buy a car if you can't get into it.'

'Let's get out of here,' I bit my lip and swallowed my urge to cry. *I feel humiliated.*

Following me out of the dealership's showroom, Dad said, 'That guy has no idea what you've been through. Don't take it personally. Let's try another kind of car.'

We went to another dealership where I found a safe car that I could get myself into.

'Would you like to go for a test drive?' the friendly salesman asked.

'Yes.' I nodded my head, impressed with the safety features of the vehicle.

'Let's drive one from the lot outside,' the salesman said. He led us out of the showroom.

While I got into the driver's seat, my dad automatically opened the front passenger door to sit next to me.

'Excuse me, sir, but it's our policy for a salesperson to sit up front. Do you mind?' The salesperson was polite, but insistent.

'Yes, I mind. My daughter is recovering from an accident.' Dad's emphatic response placated the salesperson's concerns.

'Oh. Then by all means, sit up front.' He slipped into the backseat of the car.

I turned on the engine and started the car. As we pulled out of the dealership's lot, my dad said, 'You're doing great, Julie. I can't believe that you're getting your own car after a severe brain stem injury.' He winked. I knew Dad intentionally said that to get a reaction out of the car salesman. That was my dad. A mischievous sense of humor. I heard the salesman fumble for his seatbelt and quickly click it into place as I drove the car with confidence down the street. That day I purchased the means of my escape back into a life of independence.

When I returned home with the new car, I placed my purple leg brace inside the trunk as a reminder of where I had been. A reminder of where I never wanted to return.

On 1 December 1993, I officially declared independence when I signed a rental agreement and moved into an apartment, ready to live on my own and able to care for myself. Who could have anticipated the aftermath?

CHAPTER THIRTEEN

STUCK BETWEEN FLOORS: CONTEMPLATING SUICIDE

My family and friends moved me into my apartment. Mom and I went grocery shopping. How odd that such a mundane requirement for most people was another step in my independence. *I am buying groceries for my own kitchen in my own apartment! I can't believe this day has come!*

I parked the car, and we went inside. Mom pulled out a cart. I grabbed the handle and insisted, 'Mom, I can push the cart. Let me do this.'

'Sure,' she said, stepping aside. I steadied myself against the handle and pushed the cart forward. Mobility and balance. What a great feeling. As we browsed the produce aisle together, Mom said, 'This reminds me of the time when you were eight. Remember, Julie?' Even though I have heard this story a million times, I let Mom tell it again. 'We were walking in the parking lot at the grocery store in Downer's Grove when you saw an elderly man pushing ten heavy grocery carts by himself. You tugged at my shirt and said, "Mom! No one is helping him."'

'Well, I just didn't understand why the younger employees outside weren't doing the heavy pushing. That made me so mad,' I interrupted.

Mom smiled. 'Then, you insisted, "Mom, I've gotta go talk to him," and you rushed across the parking lot. I watched you walk next to him all the way up to the front of the store. When you ran back to me, I asked, "What did you say?" You said simply, "Mom, I told him he works really hard and does a great job. I just wanted him to know he's important."' Mom touched my shoulder and said, 'Even as a little girl, you already had such a big heart.'

On 5 January 1994, I turned thirty. My parents threw a surprise party for me at a restaurant. George brought me. I walked around and introduced him to the guests. I enjoyed this happy time with friends and family, celebrating the beginning of a new decade and my new life.

Most days, however, I felt that I was physically eighty years old and emotionally three. I had to relearn every bodily function like a toddler, yet the process of that requirement made me feel old. I did not have much energy to fully embrace my miraculous recovery. Dr Shea explained to me: 'Julie, you use ten times more energy than other people do for simple tasks.' I had to strenuously concentrate to do any single movement, as if my body was driving on flat tires.

The tasks at work were becoming especially difficult for me.

In February, I approached my boss and said, 'I know I'm not here full time. Why are you still paying me on a full-time salary? Why don't you start paying me an hourly wage just for the hours that I'm able to be here? I've trained my assistant. When I'm here, I'll advise her on dealing with clients that I can no longer go and visit. That would be more reasonable.' I knew this was a conversation that I needed to have with my boss. I was the ultimate professional and wanted to do what was right and fair for all parties. I was still going to my outpatient rehabilitation three times a week.

'No, no.' He looked at me and shook his head. I sensed at that moment he was going to fire me.

George and I planned a getaway to Florida. I looked forward to this time to physically get away from the stress at work and the hovering concern of my parents. Two weeks later on the Friday before my vacation, my boss called me into his office. 'Julie, things just aren't working out.' He looked at the floor.

I started crying. *Work means everything to me. I love working!*

'Toughen up, Julie. You are making me feel bad about doing this.' He looked up at me.

'You don't know what you're doing to me. What else can happen to me? I told you before. You can pay me an hourly wage.' I gasped for words in between my sobs. The memory of Dr Shea's words echoed through my mind: 'No one will insure you. Julie, you have a permanent disability.' I knew instantly the repercussions of getting fired. I would never be able to obtain medical insurance for my severe injury again. Anywhere! I would now become dependent on Social Security disability in order to obtain Medicare insurance. How devastating to accept that I was no longer able to provide the basic needs of insurance for myself.

'I'm sorry. Things just aren't working out.' He shrugged his shoulders.

I went into my office, grabbed a few personal items and left behind the one tie to my old life. *What am I going to do? I got fired! I've always exceeded expectations on performance.* That's when I personally experienced prejudice against the disabled.

God, after all I've been through, how can you let this happen? How? I just don't get it. I have no hope. It feels like you've just completely turned off the light. What am I going to do? Where am I going to go? How am I going to pay my bills? Where are you? You told me to 'go back and be happy.' Sorry, God, but this is hell.

Instead of looking at this moment as an opportunity to reach out to God and fully trust him for abundant provision, I turned inward and stirred my anger and despair.

Somehow, I managed to drive back to my apartment. I called my parents. My world was spinning out of control, and I couldn't contain my volcanic emotions. I was afraid of what I might do. Mom kept telling me, 'Everything is going to be okay, Julie. You're okay.'

'But I'm not okay,' I sobbed. Mom kept me talking. A wise strategy. I heard a knock at the door.

'Mom, someone's at my door. I can't answer it like this.'

'Go see who it is. I'll hold on.' It was so unlike her cautious nature to tell me to answer the door when I wasn't expecting anyone to come over. But she knew who would be there. It was Dad. I opened the door, and he threw his arms around me to hug and protect his youngest daughter. I soaked his shirt with my tears. For hours he listened to me scream out my frustrations. 'Let it out, Julie. Just let it out.' He repeated his words. I knew that he wouldn't let me hurt myself. I was safe.

The next day, I left Chicago and headed to a Florida beach with George. There, I read Dr Bernie Siegel's book entitled *Love, Medicine and Miracles: Lessons Learned About Self-Healing from a Surgeon's Experience with Exceptional Patients*. This comforting book discusses the importance of finding peace of mind to help the body heal. I so wanted to find that peace of mind, but I felt myself slipping into a bottomless black hole. No one could comfort me or pull me out. Not my parents. Not even George.

This place was the polar opposite of the peace I had experienced in the light. I felt that somehow my prayers were no longer being heard by God. I needed his light to shine through my utter darkness of self-doubt and self-pity.

At that point, I locked him out of my life.

After a week, I returned to the Chicago suburbs. Life felt fragile, like the broken axles of my old car.

Over a Sunday lunch, I asked a question that no parent should ever have to hear from their own child. 'Dad,' I paused, 'I just don't get it. Wouldn't it have been easier for you guys if I had just died? Why did everybody bother?'

Dad calmly said, 'Julie, let's talk. I'm not surprised that you feel that way. But if you had died, there would have been such a huge void in our lives. You are our daughter, our flesh and blood.' Mom started crying. She left the room.

'I'm sorry.' I still had not told my parents that I actually had died. *What's the purpose anyway? I'm never going to be happy again*.

Dad then looked me straight in the eyes and said, 'Don't you ever be ashamed of what's happened to you with this injury. Don't ever be ashamed!' *Words to live by*.

Then, he said something that I will always remember. Dad held me and said, 'Julie, I am your father, and I love you so much. I will not walk in front of you because you need to be the one to lead your life. I will not walk beside you because that will be your husband's place. I will, however, always walk two steps behind you to catch you in case you ever fall.'

Because of my family's deep concern about me, arrangements were made for a family counselor to meet with us. We all sat in a room, and one by one each family member discussed the impact of my accident on their lives. I felt very guilty about the pain and suffering that I caused each of them. It was too difficult to sit there and listen to my loved ones verbalize their frustrations and feelings. I felt terrible about being responsible for changing the family's dynamics and individual roles. When it was my turn to talk,

I was speechless for a moment. Finally I stood up and said, 'I've gotta get out of here.' I just wanted to run away from everything and everyone. I desperately wanted to escape. Guilt is such a heavy burden to bear.

I left the family circle and limped into the parking lot. My family ran out to find me. 'I'm just going to disown all of you and move to New Mexico!' I screamed, fumbling for my car keys. I had never even been to New Mexico, but I thought it would be a good place to hide.

'I'm just starting to put my own life back together. I'm not ready to hear how hard it has been for you.' *I already feel guilty enough, and I didn't even do anything. I just turned left.*

Mom hugged me like a protective bear. But no one could protect me from my life. I climbed into my car and drove away.

'Please be careful,' Dad shouted. 'Please, just be careful.'

I drove to George's apartment. He opened the door. I was shaking. 'I don't feel safe being by myself tonight. I'm afraid of what I might do.'

George opened his arms and held me. At last I felt safe again. I sat on his sofa for hours. My parents called his apartment to make sure I was okay, but I couldn't talk to them.

During this uncertain time, I would not even keep a bottle of aspirin in my place. I was too afraid about what I might do with it. A man in my apartment complex who suffered from a spinal injury had committed suicide by overdosing on drugs. I was shocked to actually know someone who committed suicide. His suicide seemed to heighten my concern about taking my own life. Prior to my accident, I could never imagine even contemplating such a thing. I thought about what Dr Shea had said.

I just felt stuck between floors on an elevator. I couldn't go back down to where I was before, and I couldn't go up to where I wanted to be and to where I knew in my heart that I would be one day. I actually thought about taking cyanide. A painless and bloodless act. In my mind, committing suicide was not about 'killing myself.' It was about being so hopeless at the thought of having to live the rest of my life here without the things that make me happy, and not being able to understand why the Lord brought me back to have to struggle, when it was so beautiful in heaven. I honestly tried to convince myself that I could tell the Lord that what I thought my grandmothers meant was I could go back to heaven and be happy, but I knew he wouldn't buy it. Even though I felt such distance from God at this point in my life, I could not imagine the distance I would feel from him if I took my own life. He had given me a second chance at life, albeit a life that was completely different than one I had ever known. But it was life. As difficult as it would be, I knew I was meant to be here. But I needed help.

My parents were extremely worried and decided to intervene. They called Dr Shea and made an appointment for me to see him.

When I arrived at his office, Dr Shea said, 'Okay, Julie, talk to me.'

At first, we sat across from each other at a side table in the examination room, but I couldn't remain seated. I stood and paced across the room. Pacing had always been my reaction to stress. My left leg felt like a thousand pounds, another constant reminder of how my life had changed. Dr Shea sat on his chair with his arms crossed and watched me. I burst into tears.

'Dr Shea, I was really, really sick, wasn't I?' I continued to look at the ground to watch where I stepped.

'Yes,' he answered, somewhat surprised by the question. 'There's no medical explanation why you lived and why you are functioning so well.' His gentle tone was matter of fact, yet caring. He was concerned.

'Then why didn't you just pull the plug?' I needed to know the answer. Why did Dr Shea let me live? Why did I live?

'Legally I couldn't pull the plug. In Illinois, the next of kin must make that decision. I had to put you on life support.' His voice was calm.

'What if I had been somewhere else?' Like a trapped wild animal, I continued to move within the confines of my caged life.

'Many other states let the doctors decide. Given the severity of your injuries, they might not have put you on life support.

'Then why did everyone even bother?' I stopped walking and looked at his face. He saw my despair, the sense of facing a life of overwhelming obstacles.

'It's okay to be sad and angry. You have a right to own those feelings. Look what you have been through! You didn't cause this accident. It wasn't your fault. It just happened, and yes, it happened to you.' I listened, but I was scared. I didn't know what was going to happen to me. I felt too disabled to be normal, and I felt too normal to be disabled.

He continued, 'Of course you're going to be sad. You can actually remember how you were before. It's a horrible nightmare when you reach a point and realize that you aren't who you once were.' Dr Shea continued talking and reaching out to me as if grasping my wrist with both his hands so I wouldn't plunge from the edge of life.

'You're suffering a silent epidemic. No one can understand the emotional pain that you continue to endure. On the outside, you look terrific! There aren't any visible scars of your injury. No gashes. No fractures. A closed head injury. Yet on the inside, it's a different situation. Your spirit is broken. You are depressed.'

'People say I am lucky to be alive, Dr Shea. But honestly, I don't feel lucky. I feel so disabled. My life is completely different. The driver walked away with a $75 traffic ticket, and I can barely walk.' I collapsed in a chair across from him.

'You're right. Your whole life is different. You have suffered a severe brain stem injury that 96 percent of people die from. Yet you lived. You survived.' He added, 'Julie, your accident was not only a physical event, it was a psychological one. Yes, it was and continues to be an emotionally traumatic event. But, Julie, you have to get control of those feelings and accept that you are a brain-injured person. You have to learn to become comfortable in the body that you now have.'

No one could offer a map of my new life with a sticker that says 'You are here.' I couldn't find my way. I had no compass.

'It's just that I can't believe I'm thirty years old and can't physically do the work I know how to do. No one that would have hired me before will hire me again. I can't use two hands. I can't even hold a phone and take a message at the same time. Someone took away something huge that I did well. I've always been a top performer at any job I held. And now that's gone. My health will never be at a point again to reach my professional goals. As a young person, I should be able to take my life and health for granted, but I can't. That is my reality. And now, like you said, I have to go on Social Security Disability so I can qualify for Medicare in two years because no one will ever insure me again. I feel like I've been robbed of some very basic human rights by someone who just ran a red light!'

'Yes, something horrible happened to you. Yes, you have some physical disabilities. But don't let your depression further disable you. If you want me to, I can prescribe an antidepressant.'

No! I didn't want the 'white noise' of numbness again. When I had first moved into my apartment, I had taken myself off the antidepressants. I no longer felt depressed at that point. I was living on my own.

'No, Dr Shea. I need to feel this pain. I don't want my own feelings to be taken out of my control.' I looked at the floor. My response was adamant.

'Julie, I've personally witnessed the effects of depression with several other patients. As I've told you before, suicide is not uncommon for survivors of severe brain stem injury. It happens. Typically those patients who are educated and had a good lot in life are most susceptible to suicidal thoughts. They just can't get over the hump and live with their own perceived sense of failure to meet the expectations of an able-bodied world. I'm worried about you.' His words poured through my mind with the reassurance that my feelings were normal. Suicidal thoughts are not uncommon. I looked up.

'Julie, your recovery has been amazing and can provide hope for many people. Will you consider volunteering at Loyola's trauma support group?' He appealed to the part of me that wanted to help others. That part of me was still alive. I no longer tried to release his emotional grasp as Dr Shea pulled me away from the edge of my suicidal cliff.

'What would you like me to do?' I reconnected with life. He smiled.

'I'd like for you to speak with families of survivors who are still in comas. Your story can give them much needed hope when their own situations look overwhelming.'

'Okay, I'll do that.' I felt a purpose again.

Dr Shea made arrangements for me to volunteer one night a week with Loyola's trauma support group. I would facilitate the meetings with a nurse, a chaplain and a social worker for the family members. Loyola was a refuge, and I felt safe there. *Nothing bad can happen to me inside the hospital walls. No one will fire me. No one will judge me. No one will think that I am different.*

After volunteering one evening, I talked with one of the chaplains. He was part of the trauma support team. He knew about my miraculous recovery and wanted to talk with me about it.

'You've been incredibly blessed,' he said.

'I don't feel so blessed right now.' I still didn't understand why God remained quiet and seemingly inaccessible. Where was my happiness?

'You've been through some difficult times. Here, take this book. It's about Job.' He handed me Harold Kushner's book, *When Bad Things Happen to Good People*. I took it.

'Have you ever read the book of Job in the Bible?'

'No. I've heard about him, but I've never read about him.'

'What you're going through reminds me of Job. Out of nowhere, he lost everything, too.'

That night at my apartment, I read about Job in the Bible. I've always been an avid reader, especially of non-fiction. I couldn't put it down. Job completely lost the life he knew so suddenly. *I can relate to that. People tried to tell him how to feel about everything. Friends tried to explain why something bad happened.* Job suffered. I was suffering. But Job never lost his faith. I did. I still felt lost.

Living with my invisible wound, I had to face the visible reality of a lawsuit. My Aunt Kathy DiIorio's brother-in-law, Greg Ginex, was my attorney. Since the driver's parents owned the car and lived out of state, the liabilities were limited. However, my medical bills would be covered. When I called Greg after my vacation to get an update on the final settlement, I mentioned that I had been fired. Greg could not believe it.

'Julie, excuse me. What?'

'I got fired from my job. I was told that it was not working out.'

'Your boss can't fire you for that. We have to take legal action. He fired you illegally under the Americans with Disabilities Act.'

Greg referred me to an attorney, who filed a discriminatory lawsuit under the Americans with Disabilities Act against my former employer. During a conference in the regal chambers of the federal judge, the parties agreed upon a settlement. I didn't have the strength for a trial. I just wanted it settled.

My parents left the room. They thought I was following them. I stayed in my chair, alone in the empty chambers. *I never imagined I would be part of a disability suit.* I thought of Job. My parents returned to the room.

'I'm sorry we left you. I thought you were with us,' Mom said, sitting next to me.

I nodded.

'I know this has been tough. But it's over. Let's move on,' Dad said. 'It's time for good things to happen in your life.'

I got out of my chair, and we went to lunch.

Before the lawsuit, I was already looking for another job. I consulted the classifieds and networked with former co-workers. Because of my parents' strong work ethic, I have always been the type of person who had to work, even at a young age. At sixteen, I became a cashier at a local hardware store. At seventeen, I worked at the outdoor nursery. I enjoyed the independence of making and spending my own money. I was the first one in the family to graduate from college. I was in the top 5 percent of the class. Immediately, I was placed with a large accounting firm and later moved to a large national food chain as a senior bookkeeper. Looking for more marketing experience, I joined a national cosmetics firm as an account executive and handled million dollar accounts. In order to work on my marriage, I gave up the fast lane and found a job closer to home.

Now I couldn't even find a job. A friend, however, recommended me for a sales position behind a makeup counter at a large department store. I welcomed this opportunity, even though the position was a giant step back. The manager knew I had been in an accident, but was unaware of my severe injury.

'You're hired, Julie. We're glad you're part of the team,' she said, shaking my hand.

'Great. When do I start?'

'How about tomorrow?'

'Terrific.'

For the next two weeks, I was under non-stop stress. I could ring up the transactions and slide the credit cards. But I couldn't put makeup on other people. I could only use my right hand. I was left-handed. What used to be easy was now impossible.

The sales manager soon realized that I was not able to do the makeovers. 'Julie. Let's go outside. I need to talk to you. Oh, and bring your purse.'

Here it comes. She's going to fire me. Someone must have told her how badly I was injured. 'Okay.'

We sat on a bench in a courtyard outside the store.

'I'm sorry. I didn't realize how physically difficult this job would be for you.'

'You're right. The makeovers are difficult. But I can do everything else.' Clenching my fist, I anticipated her next words.

'I've got to be fair to the other salespeople. I need everyone to do each function of the job, including makeovers.' She looked at the ground. 'I'm sorry. I have to let you go.'

Anger boiled. I trapped it. I left like a professional. I knew no other way. Inside of the car, I cried. I wished for the physical ability to scream, but the accident took that away from me, too. Instead, I yelled inside my head *Enough! This is unbelievable! How will I ever work again? Where am I supposed to go?*

I didn't give up. I had to work. I found a job as a fragrance model for a different department store. I sprayed perfume samples for shoppers. I enjoyed the personal interaction, but knew I was capable of doing more. Over the holidays in 1994, Dr Shea was shopping with a fellow neurosurgeon. Surprised to see me spraying perfume, Dr Shea said, 'Julie. It's great to see you working. How are you?'

How am I? Happy to be working. But embarrassed that I'm fragrance modeling and not doing a job of my potential and educational training. 'I'm fine.' I forced a smile.

Turning to his medical colleague, Dr Shea nudged him and said, 'This is the miracle girl I told you about.'

'Yeah, yeah, that's me.' I switched the awkwardness of the moment by using what has always come naturally to me: my humor. Spraying a perfume sample, I handed the tester to Dr Shea. 'Here. This might be your new fragrance.'

At last, my life was starting to feel unstuck. Before I could make it up to that next floor and into my future, however, I would need to confront a person from my past and deal with the source of my anger. I couldn't live with the anger anymore. Only God could give me the strength to forgive.

I cracked open the door of my heart for him. Of course he was already there, patiently waiting. He had never turned his eyes away from me. He had never left me alone. He welcomed me back into his loving arms.

CHAPTER FOURTEEN

SEARCHING FOR ANSWERS: SESSIONS WITH A NUN

During my marital struggles, I sought help from a Franciscan nun, Sister Valerie Kulbacki. Although we are different women with different lives, she provided wise counsel throughout my divorce.

She visited me at the rehabilitation hospital and even at my parents' house. Then I stopped calling her. I was trapped in all-consuming darkness. I couldn't reach for the light. Yet Sister Val didn't encroach; she would never force the light upon me. It would be my choice to return, and eventually I did. I needed to go beyond my family to find answers to some difficult questions. I picked up the phone and called her.

'Sister Val, it's Julie. I need to talk to you.' My voice sounded desperate.

'Of course. Do you want to come to my office?'

'Yes.' We hung up, and I took my first step toward emotional and spiritual recovery.

Sitting in her small office at the parish was like returning to a childhood tree house. I felt safe there. Everything was familiar, even the shelves of countless books that surrounded me. Sister Val was always giving me books to read. After my divorce, she pulled *Women Who Do Too Much* off a shelf. Before my accident, we spent many hours in her office together.

I never seemed to be at a loss for words with Sister

Val, until now. Depression can make expression disappear. However, I still couldn't acknowledge that I was depressed. All I could feel was numbness and exhaustion. On top of everything else, I couldn't sleep. The brain injury robbed me of my ability to go into a deep sleep. My body wouldn't even let me dream.

I whispered my first words: 'Why me?'

Sister Val looked at me and said, 'I don't know, Julie. I can't tell you why bad things happen. But, it's okay to feel sorry for yourself. A terrible thing happened to you.'

'I feel so hopeless.' I had lost everything. My body. My identity as a professional. My ability to function as an adult. I was angry. Overwhelmed. Why was I still alive?

'I know. It's okay to feel angry and sorry for yourself. That's a natural part of the healing process. But you can't stay stuck in depression forever. At some point, you'll need to accept what happened and move forward, just like you did after your divorce.' I heard her words, but I couldn't connect them to my feelings.

'But I feel shut out from God.' There. I did it. I removed the cork, and my darkness spewed throughout the room.

Sister Val looked straight into my eyes and said, 'Julie, God doesn't shut anyone out.'

'But he didn't let me stay, and now I'm here. And alone. And broken.' I bent my head in shame and sobbed.

'Julie, God has not abandoned you. What do you mean, he didn't let you stay?' She reached across and gave me a handful of tissues.

I blew my nose. *I guess I have to tell her. I have to let someone know.* For too long I had felt like the first astronauts who had gone to the moon and returned to earth with feelings of loneliness and isolation because no one else had experienced what they had.

Taking a deep breath, I answered. 'I was dead and went to heaven. It was so peaceful there, full of light. I started to walk toward the narrow tunnel with this intense light flowing through it, but my grandmothers stopped me and wouldn't let me go there. I was so disappointed. I wanted to stay. I knew I was not physically okay. Then, this piercing and all-encompassing blue light was shining. Through me. Around me. Inside of me. I was told, "Your body will heal. Go back and be happy." And the next thing I remember is waking up from the coma.'

Sister Val didn't try to explain it away. She only listened. I was glad that I shared this experience with her. I felt safe to share my thoughts with her. However, I still felt alone.

'I wish I could have stayed in the light,' was all I could say. It was difficult putting my feelings into words and concepts that could be understood.

'I am sure you wish you were still there,' Sister Val said.

'It's just that I felt so close to God there, and now I feel separated.'

'God is with you here, too.'

I remained quiet for a few moments, trying to absorb all that had been said. I was afraid to commit suicide. I just wanted that same peace that there was in heaven. I closed my eyes and felt the warmth of the blue light. At least I could go back there in my mind when I needed that reassurance. It felt good to go back there. I had stayed away for too long.

'Do you think you still need to see me for counseling?' I asked.

'Yes,' Sister Val answered. 'This is a process and spiritual journey that will take awhile. Please consider coming back.'

I agreed and left her office. I knew I would be back. I had shared my deepest secret with her. By speaking for the first time about my experience in heaven, I opened my heart's door so God's light could once again envelop me with love. The following week, I returned for another visit with Sister Val.

'Why do you think I'm still here?' I asked.

As a professional counselor, she knew that I was suffering from survivor's guilt. Statistically, I should be dead or permanently comatose. However, I was functioning, albeit in a somewhat dysfunctional way. Why did I get to live?

'Julie, you know the answer to that question. You were chosen.'

'Chosen? Chosen for what? Why would God choose me?' Why was I given this gift of recovery when so many others die or struggle far more on a daily basis because of their disability? I don't feel comfortable with the word 'chosen.' Since working with families of brain injury survivors, I saw firsthand glimpses into what could have been my life.

It didn't bother me to ask straightforward questions like that. I remembered taking faith class at church when I was nine. When I asked the teacher how she knew God is a boy and not a girl, her face turned red as if I had said something blasphemous. She arranged a conference meeting with my parents for the next day. When my parents heard what I had asked, they were not angry. 'We've always encouraged Julie to question things,' Dad said. 'That's how she learns.'

Sister Val's voice awoke me from my daydream. 'You were chosen to receive this incredible gift of recovery.'

'But what does this mean?'

'I don't have an answer for you. However, I think you'll get answers through the choices you make in response to what happened.'

I listened. 'It's your choice,' she continued. 'You can accept the gift or not accept the gift. God gives everyone a free will. Whatever choice you make, your life will be different from what it was before. Your choices will determine your path.' I slumped in the chair. She noticed how overwhelmed I was. 'But first you must heal.'

She explained the feeling of survivor's guilt and validated the range of emotions that I was feeling. I read a powerful excerpt from Claude H. Rhea Jr's book, *With My Song I Will Praise Him*. At age thirty, he was miraculously healed from cancer. His written words spoke to me about my own experience:

> The team of specialists was mystified. Something beyond the power of medical science had occurred. As the recipient of this unexpected grace gift from God, I too, was amazed. Why should so many good people be taken by cancer and so few survive? Why suffering? Why should God seemingly supersede his own physical laws? Quite frankly, I don't have these answers. Prayer precipitated a twentieth century miracle in my body. God in his mercy heard and answered – and healed! I have come to believe that these tested truths can sustain any Christian during times of crisis:

* God is *able* in every trying circumstance of life.
* God has the *right* to allow his children to be tested in the crucible of pain and trial.
* God has an overriding *reason* for permitting us to suffer.
* God has a *reward* through the suffering experience and in the aftermath of tribulation.

For two straight years, I continued to see Sister Val on a weekly basis. At each session, I kept asking the same question: 'Why me?' And each time, she gave me the same answer: 'You were chosen to receive this gift.'

During this time, I made some important choices as I began to understand what had happened to me physically and spiritually, and to accept the gift. Throughout this whole extraordinary experience, I continued to feel ordinary. I didn't feel any more special than the person next to me. Sister Val said that humility opens one's eyes and heart to being blessed. And once you are humbled, you can never feel comfortable in feeling prideful again.

I realized that it would be up to me to discover God's purpose. For the first time, I didn't want to go back to who I was before the accident. Instead, I wanted to discover the person God wanted me to become. I was ready to seek the reason for my grace gift. Before that journey could begin, I called Mom at her work with some important news. I picked up the phone.

'Do you have a minute?' I asked when my mom answered.

'Of course.'

'There's something that I've wanted to share with you for awhile but didn't want it to upset you.' Mom remained quiet. 'Are you there?'

'I'm here,' she said. 'You can tell me anything, Julie. I won't be upset.'

'Well, it's about Gram. I …uh… I saw her in heaven. She looks great. And Grandma Sue was there, too.' My words jumbled together as I tried to convey this experience in the light with my mom. I didn't want to upset her, but rather to reassure her that her own mother was okay. Everything was okay. My body was starting to heal.

'This is comforting to hear.' I could hear her muffled tears. 'It means a lot to know my mother's okay in heaven. And Julie…' Her voice trembled. 'I'm so glad that you're okay.'

CHAPTER FIFTEEN

DIALING THE PHONE:
DIFFICULT CONVERSATIONS

By March of 1996, key changes took place in my life. With the proceeds from an insurance settlement, I purchased a small town home. This was a huge move for me. Not only was my injury physically disabling, but it was also financially disabling. I would never have the financial means to feel secure for life because I would not be able to work full time. However, with a background in business and an understanding of real estate, I knew that purchasing a home was financially responsible. Yes, I was frustrated that I would never be able to provide for myself in the way that I had been physically able to before, but I was no longer despondent. I knew that God would continue to provide. And he did.

Months after I was fired, God provided a part-time paying job. During 1995, I started working at Hinsdale Hospital. Although insurance would not cover pre-existing conditions, I was able to obtain a policy which would cover anything unrelated for unexpected medical emergencies.

Each day before work, I stared at the piece of paper on top of my dresser: the police report from my accident. It listed the phone number of the person who changed my life. I knew one day that I would need to confront the past in order to move forward into my future, but I had not been emotionally ready. Until now.

What had compelled me to take this drastic step? Gentle nudges from the Holy Spirit. I could no longer live with the heavy baggage of the unknown. It was time to unpack. I had to forgive. How could I forget the important lesson that I learned at age nine? Dad and I were in the family room. He was watching the evening news. I saw a man in chains. 'Who is that?' I asked.

'A murderer. He's about to be put to death for killing someone.'

'Dad, I feel really bad for that man. He's gonna die and not go to heaven.'

'We don't know that.'

'Well, he killed someone. God's not gonna let him into heaven.'

'If that man asks God to forgive him, and if that man invites Jesus into his heart, then God will let him into heaven.'

'God can forgive that?'

'Yes.'

'That's so... so unbelievable.'

'It's called amazing grace.'

I picked up the phone. I prayed and dialed the number. He answered.

'Is this Robert?' (I am not using his real name.)

'Yes, it is,' he said.

'Hello, Robert. This is Julie Papievis.'

As soon as I said my name, Robert exclaimed, 'Oh, Julie! I never knew what happened to you. You were still in the coma when I went to traffic court. No one would tell me anything. I always think about you.'

'Well, Robert, I have been thinking a lot about you, too. That's why...'

'Julie, before you say anything, I have to say something.

I am so sorry for what I did to you. I am so sorry.'

'I forgive you. That's why I called. I've waited a long time to hear myself say that to you.'

For years, we had both suffered in silence, each with our own different burdens. Finally, we had the unique opportunity to reach out and comfort each other, to help the other heal. I didn't interrupt his silence.

After a few moments, he said, 'Tell me about what happened to you.'

'Do you really want to know?' I asked, surprised by his request.

'Yes.'

'Well, I had to start over and relearn how to do everything from swallowing to standing up.'

He remained silent. I imagined this was a lot for him to hear, knowing that he was the cause. I described my rehabilitation in detail, and said that I was still going each week for physical and occupational therapy. He wanted to know, and I wanted him to know – not to punish, but to inform.

I asked, 'Don't you think it would be a good idea to include community service in a rehabilitation facility as part of a court sentence? That way, drivers can understand and experience the impact of their choices.'

'Yes, I think that would be a good idea.' His somber tone sounded well beyond his years. 'Julie, I want you to know that I'm such a careful driver now.'

'I'm glad. I'm sure you've had your own issues to deal with, too. I wish you all the best. I really do. And I will pray for you.'

'Thank you.'

'I had to call and talk to you,' I continued. 'I wanted to let you know that I'll be okay. You don't have to carry the burden of wondering what happened. God has given me an amazing grace gift. Robert, I've forgiven you, so it's time that you forgave yourself.'

We hung up. Through the act of forgiveness, any anger evaporated. My heart was ready to be healed.

One evening, I called my dad. We had always been close, and he could tell that something was bothering me.

'How are things with George?'

'Okay, I guess.' I bit my lip. 'It's pretty serious.'

'That's not a surprise – you've been dating over three years. He's okay with you not being able to have kids, right?' I was shocked by his candid question. Although Dr Shea had prepared me for the reality that giving birth and raising a child would be physically overwhelming to my body, I was still in denial. Already, I had defied medical odds in everything else. Why not childbirth? Or at least adoption?

'We haven't really talked about that,' I answered.

'Honey, George is a great guy. No doubt about that. I just want to make sure that you understand how injured your body was. You can't put yourself through the physical demands of being a mom. I know you so well, thinking that you can do this. But you can't. This could hurt you, or even kill you. As your dad, it's my job to protect you. I know this changes things for dating.'

'Dad, I appreciate your concern, but I'm old enough to decide things on my own. Especially my dating life.' His comments made me defensive, but as always, my dad's thoughts made me think. It was a tender moment to realize that motherhood was no longer an option for me, a young woman who had her own poignant dreams of being a mom.

After hanging up the phone with my dad, I thought about my nephew Clayton's christening. It had taken place almost a year ago. What an honor it was to be asked by Tammy and John to be Clayton's godmother. On the morning of this special celebration, I helped Tammy get him ready for the service. Part of the ceremony required that I, as godmother, hold Clayton as I promised to uphold my duties to teach him the ways of the Lord. Before the priest handed my godson to me, I prayed, *Father, please give me the strength to hold onto him. Please don't let me drop him.* Throughout the ceremony, Tammy and John looked over at me to make sure I didn't need any help. God was gracious and gave me strength to carry Clayton. But at that moment I knew the constant care of my own child would be too physically overwhelming.

This has been one of the most difficult dreams to let go. I really looked forward to having children. To me, that was a given in my life. I was going to have children. I wanted to be a mother. Now the reality of my loss crested and washed away one of my most cherished dreams.

A week later, I realized that there was another difficult call that I needed to make. One that would be painful. I dialed George's phone number. I owed him a great debt. He had saved my life numerous times. I depended on his strength, like the flying buttresses that support Notre Dame Cathedral in Paris. How and why should I let go of someone that I loved and depended on? In my heart I understood that true love is a selfless act, and staying with George would be selfish on my part. I thought that George's ultimate dream was to have a family. Although he might insist upon his willingness to forgo fatherhood, I couldn't let that happen. I knew if he wanted to be a father, I could not fulfill that longing. In my case, adoption was not even possible. I would never have the physical energy demanded for the basic care of a child. I could not keep the personal joy of parenting away from George. A child should have him as a father.

I called George. Perhaps I was a coward to end our relationship that way, but I didn't want him to feel obligated to stay. I was sad without him and doubted my decision. Perhaps in his own way, George realized that by letting him go, I expressed my ultimate love for him. Although wobbly without George as my flying buttress, I stood on my own by the grace of God.

CHAPTER SIXTEEN

ON WINGS OF EAGLES: RUNNING ACROSS THE FINISH LINE

In the fall of 1996, I sat on the window seat in my town home and looked outside. I envisioned myself running by my window. With determination, I whispered my heart's dream out loud: 'One day I will run again.' Although at this point I could still barely walk with good balance, an unquenchable goal brewed inside of me. I wanted to run again.

My outpatient therapy sessions continued, and I now worked part time at the Brain Injury Association (BIA). My co-workers at Hinsdale Hospital were happy for me when I accepted this new position. For once after the accident, I left a job because I chose to, not because I was fired. At the BIA, I worked part time in consumer relations, answering the phone and talking to other brain injury survivors. In addition, I coordinated their annual educational conference and assisted with other fund-raisers. The mission of BIA is to create a better future through brain injury prevention, research, education and advocacy. This association offers incredible resources and information. In Illinois alone, BIA's Toll Free Family Help line receives around 15,000 calls a year. While working there, I met someone in 1997 who was an employee at Rehabilitation Institute of Chicago. Noticing my struggle for balance in walking, she recommended that I see a specialist and referred me to Bridget Tarrant, a vestibular therapist with the Rehabilitation Institute of Chicago. I made an appointment. Noticing Bridget's running shoes, I said, 'I like your shoes. Are you a runner?' I looked at her shoes not with envy, but with hope.

'Yes,' she said. 'In fact, I'm training for an upcoming marathon, and I need to break these in.'

'Wow. You know, I used to be a runner. Just before the accident, I was training for a biathlon.' I shared this with her not to evoke pity, but to provide the basis of what I needed to ask her.

'I'm really sorry, Julie. I can only imagine how you must feel.' She looked at me with the understanding that only a runner could have about what had been taken away from me.

'Yeah, it's been tough. But I know I will run again someday. Will you help me?' There. I asked her.

'I'll do what I can, but first, let's improve your walking.' She appeared surprised to hear about my seemingly impossible goal, to run again.

Bridget evaluated the performance of my vestibular system, which is centered at the base of the inner ear. Whenever I walked and looked side to side, I would get off balance. I knew that before I could run, I would need to walk without the wobbly feeling. I was ready for the challenge. She recommended that I try tai chi through the rehab center. During my first class, I tried to balance on one leg and toppled over. Disheartened, I thought *Now what am I going to do?* Bridget then suggested that I take horseback riding lessons to improve my balance. With hesitancy, I accepted her suggestion. Although I was not an equestrian, I did have several positive experiences during childhood with horses on a family friend's farm. However, as an adult with a disability, I was afraid. Although someone walked next to the horse during the riding session, I could barely breathe, wondering what would happen if I fell off. Checking tai chi and horseback riding from my list, Bridget then recommended yoga training to stabilize my core. Finally, I found an activity that I enjoyed and could do without fear of falling. I was happy to realize that everything was done with my feet on the ground. No heights. Not only did yoga strengthen my core, it enhanced another compromised part of my body: my lungs. When I had been admitted to Marianjoy Wheaton from the hospital, I was in a coma with double pneumonia. My lung capacity remained limited whenever I breathed. Practicing yoga provided exercises to learn how to inhale properly. Breathing was essential to running. When I discussed my difficulty in balancing with my yoga teacher, she adjusted the poses that required me to stand against the wall.

At my next visit with Dr Shea, I asked, 'When am I going to be able to run again?'

He had a look of momentary disbelief and then said, 'Julie, you will never be able to run again. You experienced a severe brain stem injury. The brain stem controls breathing. That's a very important part of running. I worry about your balance, too. You could easily fall and cause further damage if you hit your head. Also, your body temperature can't regulate itself properly.'

Just hearing Dr Shea tell me that he didn't think I could do it made me more committed to knowing that I would. He still couldn't medically explain why I was even walking.

By October 1997, I was walking on the treadmill at a 3.0 speed, which was a fast pace to me. I didn't feel wobbly. Bridget was impressed. She could sense my determination and drive to be able to run one day. She contacted Dr Shea to make sure that I would medically be able to pursue running. She updated him on my progress. All he could say was, 'Bridget, let her try. If Julie thinks she can do it, she probably will.'

My goal of running began to look like a real possibility. I worked hard at maintaining my health. I consulted with someone at a local health store and started taking a regimen of various vitamins and minerals, many of which I continue today.

Five years after my accident, I purchased my first pair of running shoes. I slipped my feet into the soft leather and smiled. *Nike. At last.* The store manager suggested I take the shoes for a 'test run' outside to make sure they fit. I was walking fast on clouds. My feet felt like they could fly. I couldn't wait to physically be at the point of running.

I bought the shoes and left them on. I needed to break them in. As I walked to my car, I ran into my ex-father-in-law. Having heard and read about the progress of my recovery, he said, 'My wife and I are really happy for you, and we're proud of what you've done with your recovery.' He also told me that Bill, my ex-husband, had recently remarried. I honestly felt very happy for him. I said, 'Oh, that's great. Please give him and his new wife my best wishes.' Then I walked away on my Nike clouds, leaving behind the course of my old life.

During the summer of 1998, I started to run on the treadmill in public at Bally's Health Club. The pounding of my feet against the machine was a rhythmic beat that reverberated throughout my body, keeping time with the songs on my 'coma tape' which Brett had recorded. I was running.

Noticing my progress and commitment to running,

Bridget said, 'I think you're ready for a 5K race, Julie. Why don't you choose one to run?'

'You think I'm ready?' I was thrilled, but shocked.

'Yes, you can do this. You have stamina. Your balance is good. You've been training. Let's try it.' Her encouragement propelled me into action.

Accepting the challenge, I found a local race being held on 8 May 1999 in Downer's Grove. The date and place of this race were poignant. The date would mark six years post-accident. Throughout the years, my mom designated 10 May, the date of my accident, as 'Julie's Life Giving Day.' Each year she had called me on that date and said, 'Happy Life Giving Day!' Downer's Grove was the place where I was born and raised.

Bridget agreed to run with me on the weekends so I could get used to running outside. Prior to that, I was running only in the gym and the Rehabilitation Institute of Chicago in Willowbrook. Throughout my training, I wore a T-shirt which said 'Attitude is everything.' One of my friends had given me this shirt after I awoke from the coma. Yes, attitude is part of the equation, but gratitude is just as important. Thankfulness to God spilled over the edges of my heart.

Since I was scared at first to run by myself outside, Bridget honored her commitment and ran with me during the weekends. Bridget's assurance renewed my confidence to run alongside cars on my own. Even though I didn't feel like an Olympian, I was running! The euphoric feeling returned, and I could think with a clear head as my shoes pounded on the pavement.

However, I still held something back. I was afraid of falling. I needed to face it so I could pass it. One day, I tripped over a small crevice while jogging on the sidewalk by myself. My fall felt surreal, like it was happening in slow motion. *Dear God, please don't let me hit my head!*

A car screeched to a stop, and the female driver said, 'Are you okay? Do you need any help?'

Somewhat dazed and definitely embarrassed, I answered, 'No, I'm fine.'

'Are you sure you don't want me to drive you home?' Her voice was full of concern.

'I think I need to walk this off,' I answered, still lying on the sidewalk. 'Thanks for offering, though.'

'No problem,' she answered. 'I couldn't believe it. You were really airborne when you hit the sidewalk. I'm glad you're okay.'

I pulled myself up and waved to the woman as she drove away. Then I felt something wet on my left leg. I looked down and discovered I was covered in blood. As a result of my brain injury, I had lost the intensity of pain on my left side. I limped the remaining mile to my home, relatively pain-free. Even with this mishap, I felt ecstatic. I had faced my biggest fear about running: I had fallen, yet I got back up.

I was ready to train for a race. That night I called my parents and said, 'I ran today, and I fell.' I heard the concern in their voices and reassured them, 'I'm okay. Really. I've never felt better.' The scar on my left knee remains even today, a badge of honor.

Several months later, I fell again while I was running. My left arm was covered in blood. I went to a neighbor's place and asked for a few bandages, since I didn't have any at my home. The next day, that neighbor left a new first aid kit at my front door.

During that time, I met the paramedics who helped save my life. Dad drove me to the Lombard Fire Station. A six-foot-tall, 245-pound, jovial man walked out of the building. He extended his hand, 'Hi, I'm Greg Sauchuk. I can't believe you're here.'

'I'm Julie. But I guess you already know that.'

'How can I forget? It's amazing to see you walk and hear you talk. When we all last saw you, it looked hopeless.'

He filled in my lingering questions about the accident and introduced me to the other paramedics: Al Green, Tony Pascolla, Randy Diecke, Jim Streue. Everyday heroes. I thanked them.

'So, you're surprised I recovered?' I needed to know the answer. They knew the real critical nature of my injury.

'Definitely,' Greg said. 'When we got you to the ER, you had urinated out every bit of fluid in you and started agonal breathing.'

'What exactly is that?' I asked.

'The body's last breaths,' Al Green said.

'Thank goodness my buddy Tom Otake happened to be a block away getting his tires fixed when he heard the crash.' Greg said.

'Who's Tom?' I asked.

'He's a paramedic in Downer's Grove who was off duty that day. He somehow climbed into your car and lifted your neck to clear an air passage.'

'Yeah,' Al jumped in. 'He got oxygen to your brain and prevented further brain damage.' Al looked at me and smiled. 'Your middle name should be Hope.'

Dad and I looked at each other. *God never turns his eyes*.

On 8 May 1999, I ran in the race in Downer's Grove. It was Mother's Day, six years after my accident. No fences. No ramps. No locked doors. Only roads.

Television cameras zoomed in. WGN, the *Chicago Tribune*, and the *Daily Herald* were covering the event. I never thought I would be newsworthy, but I didn't mind sharing my story with others. The media relations area from Loyola Hospital had contacted them. However, before I felt able to share my story and gift, I needed to cross the finish line.

Mom sensed my anxiety. She hugged me and whispered, 'Julie, you're about to run a race. Do you see yourself running in this race?'

'Yes.' I ran in place to loosen my body and soothe my nerves.

'Do you see in your mind all of your family and friends that are here to support you?'

'Yes.' I envisioned all of the important people in my life cheering for me on the side of the streets.

'Do you see yourself crossing the finish line? Do you see yourself completing the race?'

'Yes, I see it happening.' I nodded and knew that I would finish the race.

'You'll do just fine. Have fun!'

Then off I went to the starting line. Someone yelled, 'Runners, ready!'

Yes. I am ready to begin my life again.

'Runners, set!'

Yes. I am set for the physical challenges that are still ahead of me.

'Go!' The gun fired.

I raced past the cameras and heard the echo of cheers from friends, family and strangers. Bridget and a Loyola trauma neurosurgeon ran by my side to monitor my breathing and to catch me if I fell. I crossed the finish line in thirty-one minutes. I completed the race.

Now I was *ready* to accept and unwrap this incredible grace gift from God. I was *set* to discover his purpose for me in life. And off I did *go* with 'wings of eagles' onto the new course of my life that God prepared for me. I was ready to tell the world: Look at me, I can run! Look at the miracle God has done!

'But those who hope in the Lord will renew their strength. They will soar on wings like eagles; they will run and not grow weary, they will walk and not be faint.' (Isaiah 40:31)

CHAPTER SEVENTEEN

UNWRAPPING THE GIFT: THE PURSUIT OF HAPPINESS

Sister Val sat in her office, waiting for me to say something. Seven years after my accident, I continued to see her for counseling.

'What do you think he wants me to do now?' I had run the 5K race. What was next?

'What do you think?' she asked.

'I don't know.' I shrugged my shoulders.

'I think you know the answer to your own question.' She always expected me to find answers to my own questions, and somehow I always did.

'Well, after I woke up from the coma, I did make a promise to God. I told him that I would work hard to help my body recover so one day everyone would know about him.' I thought about that day in Marianjoy when I shared this with the priest. At that point in my life, my purpose seemed futile and far away. Yet God knew all along the plans he had for me.

'Are you ready to share his story?'

'Almost. I just don't know how.' I shrugged my shoulders.

'God will show you.' Sister Val spoke with profound assurance. 'Just be willing and ready.'

Being a deeply private person, I knew it would be difficult

to expose my vulnerability, but I was willing and ready. I wanted to honor him.

The Mother's Day race was a catalyst for more changes in my life. In 2000, I was asked to become a member of the Advisory Board for the Midwest Brain Injury at Clubhouse, a not-for-profit organization in Chicago, Illinois, which offers adult brain injury survivors the daytime experience of independence with the help of volunteers. Daily activities at the Clubhouse include answering telephones, writing newsletters, learning employment skills, cleaning, working on school assignments, making special arts and crafts projects and interacting with other survivors.

After running in a race sponsored by the Clubhouse, I talked to Dr Norton Flanagan, a neurosurgeon at Lutheran General and a board member of the Clubhouse. He was amazed at the miraculous nature of my recovery. It defied medical explanation. This amazement is a constant reaction from those within the medical community who understand the full impact of a severe brain stem injury.

'Julie, are you out speaking? People need to hear your story. You need to give people hope,' Dr Flanagan said.

Tony Romanucci, the board president of the Clubhouse, who was standing next to Dr Flanagan, agreed. 'Julie, you need to share your story.'

The next day, Tony called and asked if I would consider joining his law firm, Romanucci & Blandin, in Chicago. Aware of my limitations when it came to holding a full-time position, he offered me a part-time opportunity to be the firm's community relations advisor.

'Julie,' Tony said. 'This will give you the chance to meet with other survivors and their families and also give you the time to work on writing your book. I feel that a book will open doors for you to speak to others about surviving a traumatic brain injury.'

I was elated: God provided. At that point, I was not ready to write a book, but I was eager to start the new job. As community relations advisor, I share information about different resources and organizations that can help the survivors and their families. In addition, I talk candidly about living with an injury, yet at the same time I share the message of hope – that they too can get through this sudden change and find a new path.

One evening after work, I noticed the flashing light on my answering machine. I played the message: 'Hello, this is a producer from Lifetime Television for Women. Please give me a call.'

I listened again and then picked up the phone. Lifetime wanted to feature my story on the show, *Beyond Chance*. They had read an article about me in *Woman's Day* magazine. Someone had called the national headquarters of the Brain Injury Association to inquire about survivors beating the odds. I felt humbled and honored that *Woman's Day* chose me as part of their feature in the 1 November 2000 issue. I never realized that this article would open the doors to additional coverage. I felt grateful for another opportunity to share my story with others.

I was glad, however, that the Lifetime producer didn't know about the photo shoot for the *Woman's Day* article. While I was in the backseat of a limousine, heading to Chicago for the photo location, I had felt sick. There was no coffee can. I threw up.

In October 2001, Lifetime Television featured my story. I will never forget watching the segment with Dr Shea getting filmed. Many of us in the room cried as he discussed the severity of my brain stem injury and tried to explain the inexplicability of my miraculous recovery. Describing his amazement at seeing his 'dead patient' at my first follow-up visit, he said, 'I couldn't believe it! She was alive, and she was thinking, and she was talking. If you look at Julie's comeback, truly there are other forces at work that we don't understand at all.'

As a result of my injury, I have become friends with some very special people, including Mary. She used to be a nurse. One of her patients brutally beat her in the hospital. She faced a long recovery and has relinquished her dream of continuing a successful career in nursing. Yet through this injury, Mary's spiritual strength has remained intact, and she discovered a new path. From prisons to schools, Mary shares her faith and her tragic experience with others to encourage them to find solace through God.

Ricky also became a dear friend. He, too, had been beaten and suffered a stroke. He was a special person. His death in 2003 was another reminder that the lives which traumatic brain injury does not take instantly are often taken too soon.

Many brain injury survivors also suffer from spinal cord injuries. Dr Shea introduced me to the director of the Spinal Cord Injury Association of Illinois. Through this association and their ThinkFirst Program, I have spoken to schools around the Chicago area to educate students about driving safely. The American Association of Neurological Surgeons (ANS) and the Congress of Neurological Surgeons (CNS) implemented the development of ThinkFirst, an international program, due to their frustration at not being able to cure or "fix" brain and spinal cord injured patients. These groups share the belief that prevention is the only cure. My constant message to the middle school and high school students is to be responsible. I am an example of what can happen if they run a red light.

After a speech, a young girl approached me and wanted to talk. Something had happened to her uncle, and he was in a coma from an aneurism. While we were talking, she reached out to touch my left hand. She wanted to understand what paralysis felt like. Children often try to tangibly understand this abstract concept, and it's difficult to explain. When I awoke from my coma, it was as if my left side had been sealed inside a concrete sidewalk. Physical heaviness and immobility.

One of the best parts of my gift is to share my story with other survivors through speeches and one-on-one meetings.

'Does anyone ever feel like they just want to run away?' I asked a group of adult brain injury survivors at the Midwest Brain Injury Clubhouse.

Looking at my fellow survivors, I noticed that everyone raised his or her hand. I knew what I needed to say.

'There was a time in my life when I wanted to run away to New Mexico. I've never even been there. It's a place where I thought that I could hide. I was so frustrated, living inside a body that just didn't feel or work like the one I had before. Everything was too overwhelming for me – the therapy sessions, living with my parents, trying to be independent, and realizing that my life would never be the same. I felt lost. Do you ever feel that way?'

'Yes!' An audible wave of relief passed throughout the group. Relief that someone else was experiencing those same unspoken thoughts. These survivors were not alone in their feelings.

'Just because our lives drastically changed doesn't mean that who we are inside changed, too. Right?' Nods again.

'We all still have the same – if not deeper – emotions, hopes and dreams. Some of us may be physically disabled, but we're not emotionally disabled. During my recovery, my neurosurgeon, Dr Shea, gave me the best advice. He said, "Julie, you need to accept that you are now a brain-injured person and learn how to become comfortable in the body that you now have." That is a huge deal. Acceptance took a long while for me. When I did accept my new life, I was able to move forward and find my own special purpose. Everyone has a special purpose and a unique gift to share with others. Remember that, okay? You all have a special purpose.'

I opened *The Purpose Driven Life*, a book by Rick Warren that many of the members had expressed an interest in reading. I read from the first page of the book. 'It's not about you. The purpose of your life is far greater than your own personal fulfillment, your peace of mind, or even your happiness. It's far greater than your family, your career, or even your wildest dreams and ambitions. If you want to know why you were placed on this planet, you must begin with God. You were born *by* his purpose and *for* his purpose.'

After the session, a young man tentatively approached me with his completed art project. Handing me a dangling, metal butterfly, he presented the gift. 'Julie, this is you. You're a butterfly now.' Blinking back tears, I smiled, accepted the gift, and hugged the young man. *Thank you, God, for healing my broken wings. Through your grace, I can fly away from my cocoon.*

Recently I followed a professional coordinator into a therapy room at Rehabilitation Institute of Chicago, where I am a volunteer in the Peer Support Program. 'This is a young girl who was in a car accident,' the coordinator explained.

I approached the young girl. *She's only in her early twenties. How tragic.* She was strapped onto a slant board. Unresponsive. Vulnerable. One eye swollen shut, the other eye barely open.

I felt like I was looking in the mirror of my past at Marianjoy. I leaned close and said, 'Hi, I'm Julie. I know you're in there. I've been there before too. You won't always be stuck. One day you'll be able to tell us what you're thinking.'

She opened her good eye. She smiled.

Chapter Eighteen

Writing a Book: The Voice of My Heart

While working at the Brain Injury Association, I had an opportunity to meet with a neuropsychiatrist and share my story with him. During our conversation, I said, 'Everyone keeps telling me this recovery is so unusual, and they've never seen anything like it. I keep hearing that I should write a book. What do you think? Is my recovery really that unusual?'

'Your recovery from this injury is what people would look like if they lived. But they don't.' His demeanor was serious and professional. Finally I got it. My story needed to be told, but I knew I couldn't write it.

Dr Shea, he said, 'Julie, people need to hear you. People need to learn never to give up. Your voice can help break the silence of this silent epidemic. I am now able to say to other patients and their families that I have seen firsthand an incredible recovery from a traumatic brain injury. That gives them hope.'

His words triggered a memory. The little boy tugging at the covers of my bed in Marianjoy and saying, 'My mommy's sleeping.' I recalled what I had said to my mother: 'One day, I want to be the voice for people who cannot speak.' That was another purpose of my gift – to share with others the trapped feelings that their loved ones experience after a traumatic brain injury.

143

As a private person, I struggled with the transparency and vulnerability that writing a book would involve. Since my accident, I feel that I've been carrying around this huge secret – not only about my visit in heaven, but also about how disabled I really am. The overwhelming effects of an injury are not always apparent to someone on the outside. One might look at me and wonder, 'Why is she parking in a handicapped parking spot? She doesn't look disabled. She is even walking.' If those people only knew what a moment in my head felt like, they would understand. Every second that I am not lying down, I have to consciously battle vertigo. My life is no longer effortless. It's an effort to walk straight. It's an effort to coordinate every muscle in my body to work together. It's an effort to be healthy and alive. By writing a book, I am opening myself up so others can better understand the struggles and daily life of people with traumatic brain injuries.

Realizing the scope of this project, I surrendered it to God. 'God, if you want this to be a book, please introduce me to someone who can write it. Help me know who that person is supposed to be. Let this project honor you so everyone can know how wonderful you are.' Before undertaking such a huge task, I needed the blessing not only of God, but also my parents. This was their story, too.

My dad is also intensely private, and I knew this book might make him uncomfortable. I was surprised by his response. 'Julie, your story has to be told. A cleaning lady at work even said that. She told me that so many people had been praying for you, and that God heard the prayers. Your story is a miracle. People need to know that. So let me know if there's anything you need from Mom and me. We're here for you.'

I have always been very close to my dad's sister, Kathy

DiIorio. She and her husband Peter, along with their sons, have all been supportive during the whole process of my recovery. One afternoon she called and asked if I wanted to have lunch with her and her friend Margaret McSweeney. They lived in the same town, and Margaret had interviewed me a few weeks before for an article in a suburban newspaper.

We decided to meet at a restaurant in Oak Brook Mall. Margaret introduced herself and exuded a professional yet personable demeanor. During lunch, I shared with her more details about waking up from the coma. When I said, 'To this day, I don't understand why I asked the nurse what happened to my yellow Toyota. I never even owned a yellow Toyota, and I sure don't know anyone with a yellow Toyota,' Margaret appeared as if she were about to choke on the salad and she took a sip of iced tea.

'Julie, my first car was a yellow Toyota.' In that moment, we both sensed that God was tapping us on the shoulders. We were meant to meet each other.

After coffee and dessert, I hugged Margaret good-bye and asked, 'Would you consider writing my book?'

'I'll pray about it.' Margaret smiled and left the restaurant. 'We'll be in touch.'

The next day she called. 'I feel like this is something I'm supposed to do,' she said. 'I've prayed about it and talked with my agent. I want to be the voice of your heart.'

And so it began. A friendship and a book.

For months, we would meet once a week while her daughters were in school. She drove forty minutes to my house and asked questions, recorded sessions and took notes. She was a former banker and wanted to be meticulous in gathering the facts and understanding the timeline. She interviewed the doctors, the paramedics, the firemen, the trauma nurse, Sister Val, my family, my friends and many others.

Writing a book has been very difficult for me. First of all, I am an extremely private person. This intimate exposure of examining my life, my thoughts, my emotions and my personal faith is humbling. Margaret has peeled off the layers of my life experiences to reveal what I was and who I became by the grace of God.

Also, it is painful to relive the dark moments of my depression and speak candidly about them. When Margaret asked me to review the chapter about my suicidal behavior, I read the pages and wept. *That was me. How could that have been me?*

Throughout this process, however, I can honestly say, This is not about me! This book – my story – is written to honor God and to share this miraculous recovery with others. To give people hope and reassurance that God loves us. He is with us during our most difficult times.

Recently, while riding the commuter train to work in Chicago, I sat next to a priest. For some reason, I felt compelled to share my story with him. Intrigued by the miracle of my recovery, the priest insisted, 'You must include Isaiah 41:13 in your book.'

The verse in Isaiah reads, 'For I am the Lord your God, who takes hold of your right hand and says to you, Do not fear; I will help you.' Isn't that an amazing thought and reality: God holds our hand!

Through her research, Margaret discovered the full name of one of the witnesses at the crash: Toni Rapach. Margaret wanted to speak with her about details of the accident. Searching online for a phone number, Margaret called her and left a message. 'Hi, this is Margaret McSweeney. I'm trying to reach Toni. I'm writing a book on behalf of Julie

Papievis. I believe you witnessed her accident over a decade ago. Could you please call me?'

I will always remember meeting Toni for the first time. We met at her house. Although we were strangers, we hugged each other and cried.

'Are you okay? Are you really okay?' She clung to me.

'I'm fine. Really,' I reassured her.

'But it was so violent. I watched that car crash into you, and I felt so helpless. And hopeless. It was such a bad accident, and it was you. I can never get the picture of you when I ran to the car out of my head. I thought you were dead. It changed my life forever.'

CHAPTER NINETEEN

TESTING THE WATERS: A US OLYMPIC SWIM COACH

During 2006, I joined Advocate Good Samaritan Health and Wellness Center. I enjoyed using the facilities and taking exercise classes there.

In the lobby, large windows overlook the award winning pool. The place was unusually busy and crowded one day. It looked like a swim meet of some sort. Pressing my forehead against the glass, I watched the swimmers. They looked graceful as their arms lifted above them in a freestyle stroke. Turning their heads in a choreographed manner, they took a breath as they kicked their legs to propel their bodies forward. I missed the feeling of being completely submerged and surrounded by water.

When I was a child, Dad put a pool in the backyard. Each summer, he required anyone that wanted to play in the pool to swim at least two laps. He wanted to make sure our friends knew how to swim and that they didn't need a flotation device. My childhood summers consisted of swimming in the backyard and enjoying outdoor picnics with family, friends and neighbors. I was a mermaid. And now I was afraid to stick my toe in a swimming pool.

Diane Ahern, head of marketing, walked by and approached me. 'Hey, Julie, you should be doing this.'

'What's going on?' I asked.

'It's the annual indoor triathlon.' She was always encouraging me to get involved in the various activities and events sponsored by the center.

'I can't do that.' I looked at her and then looked back at the pool. 'I'm afraid to get in the water. I don't know if I can swim.'

'We could make some accommodations for your disability, but we also have a personal trainer who will work with you on relearning how to swim. She's been trained to teach people with disabilities.'

'I don't know if I can afford to do that right now. I live on Social Security.' The idea of a personal trainer teaching me how to swim again intrigued me. But as always, so many great opportunities came down to what it would cost. As someone living on limited income, I had to focus my funds on the essentials in life, not the dreams.

'Don't worry, I'll make some arrangements,' Diane said. I didn't know how to answer.

'Thank you' was all I could say.

A week later, I was in the locker room, trying to cool off after my workout on the treadmill. Bending over, I held a hair dryer over my mop of hair. I heard someone laugh and ask, 'Is there a person under that head of hair?'

Looking up, I saw two women and laughed. 'Hi, I'm Julie.'

'So you're Julie. You're the one who had the horrible accident. I understand you want to get back into the water. Diane signed you up for some sessions with me. I'm Carol.'

'And I'm Angie,' the woman next to her said.

'It's nice to meet both of you.' I wrapped my hair in the towel. 'Will each session cost a lot? I told Diane that I can't afford it.'

'I want to do this for you.' I didn't know what to say.

'Just let me do this for you.' The generosity offered from another person's heart is humbling.

The next week was my first swimming lesson. Eager and committed to this next challenge, I arrived forty-five minutes early. Carol led me to the therapy pool, which was small and only 3½ feet deep. As we walked down the pool's steps, Carol held onto one of my elbows and I held onto the rail. She helped lead me to a corner of the pool. The water felt like a bathtub, and most of my body was well above it.

'Hold onto the railing and start bending your knees to get your head closer to the water.' Carol showed me the rail located beneath the edge of the pool's wall. Touching the edge, I touched a memory. I was in high school, volunteering for a Special Olympics event. My job was to stand at the edge of the pool and cheer for a little boy. 'You can do it! You can do it!' I encouraged him. When he finished the race, I helped him out of the pool and handed him a towel. 'You did a great job,' I said, and then led him to his parents. Now, here I was by the edge of the pool, trying to garner the courage to learn how to swim again.

'Touch your chin to the water and blow bubbles. You can do it.' Carol held onto me so I wouldn't be afraid.

I was able to do what she asked. In a calm voice she instructed me: 'Okay, just take a deep breath and put your head under the water.'

'No, I can't.' I gripped the rails and exploded into tears. I wasn't afraid of dying. I was afraid of drowning. My severe brain stem injury deleted the ability to determine where my body was in space. If I went under the water, I wasn't confident that I would know how to get back to the surface. Also, with my compromised lungs, I didn't know if my body would know not to suck in the water. I didn't trust myself. My body wasn't working right.

'That's okay,' Carol reassured me. 'Now I know where we need to start.' She reached across the edge of the pool and grabbed goggles and a snorkeling tube. 'Here. The goggles will help you see where you're going, and the tube will help you breathe.' She helped attach the gear around my head.

'Now, try putting your head under the water.' I could feel her strong arms supporting my body. I felt safe, and submerged my head. Immediately, she pulled me back to the surface.

'Great job. Now go a little farther down this time.' I took one deep breath and went beneath the surface. I do not have the lung capacity of Japan's women divers who hold their breath to dive to the ocean's floor to seek treasures from the sea. However, I appreciate each breath I am able to take. How absolutely amazing that God breathed life into us! Each breath we take is truly a divine gift from our Creator. Carol lifted me back to the surface. I didn't drown.

During the next session, Carol wanted me to start doing laps in the therapy pool. 'Show me your freestyle, Julie.'

With my goggles and snorkeling tube attached, I reached my right arm over my head. My left side wouldn't reach as far and my body flipped too far to the side. However, I didn't panic, since my snorkeling tube provided a way to breathe. As I pushed myself to keep trying, my brain began to reconnect with my body. I was remembering the feeling of how to swim. Just like my dad made me swim laps in the backyard pool, Carol was encouraging me to swim laps in the therapy pool. 'You can do it, Julie. You're doing great!' I was swimming.

Soon after I started working with Carol, she attended a swim instructor conference in Oak Brook that was led by an internationally known swim coach, Milt Nelms. He is considered to be a master of form and has worked with some of the world's top Olympic swimmers. At our next session, Carol said, 'Oh, by the way, I shared your story with Milt Nelms, and he wants to see you swim on Saturday.'

'What? Why would someone like him want to see someone like me? In case you hadn't noticed, I'm not an Olympic swimmer,' I laughed.

'He knows that. Milt is great. He enjoys working with people who have disabilities and helping them achieve their goals.' Carol held her clipboard to her side.

That Saturday we met at the hotel where the conference was being held. Milt was standing by the pool watching some of the conferees. Carol walked by my side. This famous swim coach extended his hand. 'Hi, I'm Milt. Julie, I'm glad you could come over. Go ahead and get in the water.'

My mouth dropped. I looked at the Olympic size pool. It was much larger than the small, rectangular therapy pool at the fitness center. And where were those wonderful rails on the edge that I could hang onto?

'I'll help you with your gear.' Carol tightened the goggles and adjusted the snorkeling tube. 'You can do it.' She helped me get into the water.

'Okay, Julie, swim for me. Start with the freestyle,' Milt instructed.

I looked at the length of the pool. *It's a million miles away*. I extended my arms and started to swim. All I could do was pray and swim. *Thank you, God! I can't believe I'm swimming in front of a famous swim coach*. Through my goggles I noticed the silver-haired man with broad shoulders watching my swim technique and taking notes. He reminded me of my dad, who was also silver-haired. This similarity relaxed my racing mind. I concentrated on lifting, kicking and breathing. After swimming a million miles, I reached the edge of the other side.

'Okay,' Milt leaned over. 'Go ahead and swim back.' *He's got to be kidding, right? Swim another million miles back? I miss that therapy pool.* This was my once in a lifetime opportunity to swim for someone like Milt. I didn't hesitate to head back to the other side. While swimming the second lap, I felt a sharp tingling sensation from my left shoulder to my fingertips. It was the same intensive feeling I had in my toe at Marianjoy. Could it be that something more was happening to my body, or did I hurt it? I pushed these concerns away and focused on the task at hand.

'Your form is not that bad. It's obvious you swam before,' Milt encouraged me from the edge of the pool. I could sense his sincerity and genuine interest in helping me achieve my best performance. I incorporated his suggestions on my technique and form to improve my strokes. He gave me hope.

As I left the pool, Milt said that he wanted to continue helping me. Although he lives in Australia, he suggested Carol and I send videos via e-mail to show my progress. Exhausted, I shook his hand and stepped away with the assurance that God was leading me where I needed to go. My left side continued to tingle.

When I phoned Dr Shea with the news about the tingling, he was encouraged. 'Julie, that's great. The tingling means that your neurotransmitters have found new ways to connect.' His words reminded me of my promise to God that I would work hard for the best possible physical recovery so everyone will know his story and amazing gift of grace in my life.

CHAPTER TWENTY

TRAINING FOR A TRIATHLON: A DREAM QUEST

During one of my first swim sessions, Carol said something that I never dreamed would become a possibility in my life. As I was stepping into the large pool, she said, 'Julie, you are an athlete with natural ability. You should consider doing the indoor triathlon at the center next year.'

'Me? A triathlon?' I looked at her and laughed.

'Yes.' Carol's face was serious. 'Just because something happened to you doesn't mean you stopped being an athlete. You can do a triathlon. It's a mindset.' Her encouraging words were a soothing balm.

'But I can't swim that long.' A triathlon seemed impossible.

'You only have to swim for ten minutes, and you've already done that. You swam for Milt for that length of time. You can do this,' Carol encouraged. She was right.

'I'm going to try something today,' Carol said. 'While you do the freestyle, I'll walk in front of you and see if the water movement helps propel you forward. Jina, would you mind standing in front of the handicap access area so Julie won't swim into it?'

Pushing off the wall, I began to swim freestyle. When my hand hit against something hard, I lifted my face out of the water. I thought I had hit the side of the pool. That's when I noticed that Carol's lip was bleeding. Mid-stroke, I had accidentally pounded her. I was swimming faster than she was walking.

Taking the tube out of my mouth, I apologized. 'Are you okay? I'm so sorry!'

'Look at how much strength you have. You can do a triathlon,' Carol laughed.

Carol asked me to join her Masters' Swim Group in addition to my private swim lessons. She divided the pool into designated lanes. One lane was for the advanced swimmers, another was for the triathlon participants, and another was for people like myself who were considered beginners. To help me focus solely on the form of my arms, Carol put fins on my feet, paddles on my hands and a snorkeling tube in my mouth. The fins propelled me forward, and the hand paddles were like fins for the hands, allowing me to build strength in my upper body. For this hour-long class, I swam and swam and swam. Once again, I felt like a mermaid, splashing through the water.

Since the Masters' Swim Group was also about mastering other strokes, she approached me and said, 'Here, hand me your snorkeling tube and try the breaststroke. It's the most complicated stroke, but I think you can do it.'

Reluctantly, I handed her my breathing tube. I took a deep breath and plunged below the surface. Like a sea turtle, I pulled myself back to the surface and took another breath. This stroke felt natural to me. Don't ask me to skip or square dance, but I could do the breaststroke. It was effortless. After completing a lap, Carol looked at me and said, 'You got it! You have such a good feel for the water. That's the stroke you'll do for the triathlon!' My senses were heightened in that area, and I could do that stroke. I could feel the texture of the water.

The triathlon would require ten minutes of swimming, twenty minutes of stationary biking and fifteen minutes of running. Angie, a businesswoman, offered to become my triathlon partner on our team, which would also include Laura, a paralegal, and Jina, also a businesswoman. The fact that these women wanted me to be part of their team made me feel special, but beyond that, they made me feel that I belonged.

Most disabled people say they want to be treated like everybody else, and they mean it. If people only knew what a huge deal it is for someone who is disabled to feel just like everybody else. They just want to be included and to belong.

Throughout my recovery, I have never been treated like someone who can't do something. Family, friends, doctors and even most therapists were always positive, saying, 'You can do it.' Of course my ability and agility to 'do' was limited, but I was still encouraged and never told 'you can't' – except of course by the nurse who told me not to get out of bed after waking up from a coma because I couldn't walk. Recovery is physical and mental. Hearing positive reinforcement makes a tangible impact.

I committed myself to the challenge of participating in a triathlon and surrendered it to God. *Lord, if you want me to do this, please provide the strength.*

Carol was thrilled about my commitment to participate. A disabled person had never taken part in this indoor triathlon before. She hoped that my participation would be an inspiration for others to attempt a triathlon.

My former athletic self was determined that I wouldn't be the 'weakest link' of my team. I was ready to focus all my energy and strength to prepare for this event. Angie and I trained for running both on the indoor track and outside in the forest preserves. By running with Angie, I was able to pace myself at a higher speed. She would make me talk even though I wanted to just listen to my tunes on the headphones. By making me speak, Angie knew that my breathing was under control. I enjoyed sharing with her the progress of the book. She was very supportive.

To prepare my legs for the cycling, Angie suggested that we ride a tandem bike. At first I was hesitant. Only months ago, I had tried to ride a regular bike for the first time since my accident. What a humbling, or rather humiliating, experience that had been. A friend and I rented bikes and pedaled along a gravel bike path in Geneva. My balance felt unstable, but somehow I was able to remain on the bike. Noticing a slight turn in the path, I tried to steer the bike to the right. 'Turn! Turn!' my brain yelled to my arms, but nothing happened. Thankfully, I was able to slow down the bike before falling over into some shrubs. At least they didn't have thorns. Of course I was wearing a helmet, so my head was not injured. I was okay, but the bush was injured, along with my confidence to ever get back on a bicycle again.

'Julie, I'll balance the bike. Don't worry. It will be great strength training for our legs.' Angie convinced me. I could trust her.

She graciously rented the tandem at a bicycle store in Geneva, and we rode along a bike trail. Thankfully, it was a different trail than the one I had been on during my bike crash. Angie rode in the front of the bike and kept us balanced. With my strong legs, however, I was able to help propel the bike forward.

Swimming became a natural part of my life. In fact, Carol asked me to help teach the breaststroke to others. The simplest way I instructed people was to just fall into the water and pull themselves back up. I no longer had a fear of drowning. As I swam, I did calculations in my head.

I thought about a sweater that I wanted to buy. It had been discounted by 20 percent during a sale, so I calculated the new price in my head.

The goal of completing the triathlon became tangible and realistic for me. As I pedaled forward, I thanked God for this incredible opportunity.

CHAPTER TWENTY-ONE

AN UNEXPECTED DEATH: SAYING GOOD-BYE TO MY PAST

My life settled into a comfortable pattern. Two days a week I worked at the law firm. In between, I scheduled speaking engagements, volunteered at rehabilitation centers and worked with Margaret on the book. In the evenings, I trained for the triathlon. My mental focus was strong and my physical strength was intact. Who could have imagined the spiraling effect a phone call would have on my sense of normalcy?

'Julie, I have something to tell you.' Mom's voice sounded serious and almost hesitant. I had just returned home from work and was eating dinner. Instinctively, I put down my fork, preparing myself for what she needed to say. 'I have some very bad news that I need to tell you.'

My mom is not a dramatic person. I knew someone must have died. *What's coming next?*

'Honey, Bill passed away.' A pin pricked my balloon. My ex-husband was dead. I exploded into tears. 'Julie, I'm sorry. I should have come over to tell you the news. I should be there with you.' He had died from kidney and liver failure. Bill was only forty-seven years old.

I couldn't catch my breath. I just sobbed. After hanging

up with my mom, I picked up the phone and called Sister Val. She had been trained as a grief counselor.

'Julie, I'm so sorry.' She consoled me on the phone. She knew Bill. In an attempt to save our marriage, I had asked Bill to come to some counseling sessions with Sister Val. Each time, he would get so upset and would leave in the middle of the session. We wanted our marriage to work, but there were some serious problems to overcome. All the feelings of guilt and sorrow about our failed marriage gushed through my mind. I couldn't stop crying. All I could do was listen to Sister Val.

'I want you to have peace about this. You know where Bill has gone. He's a believer. Have faith in that. I know how hard this is, but you have to let yourself grieve. You haven't had time to grieve the divorce, and now you have to grieve his death, too. You'll work through all of this. You always do, Julie. But let yourself cry. That's okay. You loved each other. He will always be an important part of your life. Let the tears flow.' She continued to comfort me over the phone for a long time. That night, and several nights after, I cried myself to sleep.

The following week was Bill's wake. I never doubted that I would go. I just wasn't expecting to go there alone. My parents were at a wedding, and my best friends Jill and Sue had plans that couldn't be changed. My triathlon teammates offered to go there with me, but I declined their offer. They insisted, however, on taking me out to dinner after the wake. I agreed to that offer, knowing that after such an emotional experience, I would need to be in the company of friends.

Dressed in black, I walked into the funeral home and signed the guest book. His mother approached me and hugged me tight. 'Julie, I'm glad you're here. We're proud of the kind of work you're doing. You're helping so many people.' I appreciated her kind words. I saw his father standing at the casket, and I walked toward him. As we were talking, I noticed a woman standing to the side. I thought that this might be Bill's wife. She walked up to me. I was afraid of how she was going to feel about my being there. 'Julie?' I nodded. 'You belong here. You were such a big part of his life for such a long time.' She hugged me, and we both cried in each other's arms. I appreciated her graciousness. She was right. Bill was an important part of my life. We had shared eleven years together.

Looking back at the casket, I knew what I had to do. I knelt in front of it and looked at my former husband. I didn't even recognize him. I started praying and crying. All the sudden, I stopped crying and thought, *I'm so mad at you for dying so young*. I was grateful that Bill had someone as lovely as his wife to take care of him while he was sick. My heart broke for her. My heart broke for his parents and siblings. They were the ones left behind. I knew where he was. He was in the light, in heaven. I closed my eyes and allowed the warmth of the stained glass blue light to hug my frail spirit. I was at peace. It was time to move forward, grieving the past and embracing the future. I left the funeral home and met my triathlon teammates at a restaurant.

CHAPTER TWENTY-TWO

AN ACCOMPLISHED GOAL: FINISHING THE RACE

Throughout the training process, Carol always stressed the importance of camaraderie with teammates. She wanted training to be fun and explained, 'There is a lot more to athletics than the mechanics. When you train, to have a successful program, you have to create a socialization. You have to create bonds. You have to create a reason to go out and do your training, but you also have to want to come and see your friends. If you don't have that friendship, then there's always a reason not to come. But when you look forward to camaraderie, you're more apt to follow the program and succeed.'

Carol's wisdom proved correct. My fellow teammates became close friends. We were all supportive of each other and accountable to each other. The full week before the triathlon, they brought three full meals each day to make sure I was getting the proper amount of carbohydrates and protein that my body would need. Over the course of training, I gained ten pounds!

The morning of the race, I ate a small breakfast of bananas and an English muffin with peanut butter. I was grateful that Angie volunteered to drive. At the table, I closed my eyes and prayed. *Dear God, please give me the strength to do my best and help me finish well. I do this all for you. Thank you for this recovery. Thank you for my family and for my friends. Help others see your love for them through me. Amen.* I was ready.

Seeing the familiar faces of friends and family standing around the pool encouraged me. Margaret was there with her youngest daughter, Katie, who had made a poster with a friend to cheer me on. And there were cameras, too. WGN and some local newspapers were covering the triathlon event and my participation. I just tuned them out and focused on what needed to be done: swimming, cycling and running.

The anticipation and buildup for this day made me nervous and affected my performance. During the ten-minute swim time, I was unable to complete the typical number of laps I had in practice. I could not coordinate my stroke. My rhythmic motion was off. Like Carol had said, the breaststroke is the most complicated stroke anyone can do. I had never encountered this difficulty until now. Although I had conquered my fear of drowning, my focus on competing well slipped away. My brother Brett stood at the other end of the pool and shouted encouraging words to me. 'Breathe, Julie! You can do it!' The ten minutes passed. I would need to make up my time in the next events. I had five minutes to get out of the water and get ready for the bike.

Angie and I had practiced this transition many times. I left my shoes untied with my socks in them, next to my headphones, which also served as my hair band. Holding onto the rail, I walked downstairs to the stationary bikes. The cameras followed me. I didn't worry about how I looked at that moment. There is no room for vanity in a triathlon.

On the bike, I began to pedal. Although I could have gone faster, I wanted to save strength in my legs for running. They were new bikes which arrived just the day before the triathlon. I had never practiced on one of these before. I tried to smile and speed up when I noticed the camera zoom in for a close-up. Katie waved the big poster to provide cool air on this winter day. The cool breeze helped a lot as the miles continued to accumulate during the twenty minutes of pedaling. I had biked over five miles. It was time for the next event.

Walking over to the indoor track, I felt some heaviness in my legs, but I was eager to finish strong with my running. Angie and I ran next to each other, pacing ourselves. I knew that I would be behind most everyone, but that didn't matter. I wanted to finish strong. The 80s tunes blasted in my headset as we ran around the track. A friend of mine who works in radio helped me put the soundtrack together. It was like high school reunion with the familiar tunes from my teenage years. Toward the end of the race, I could no longer feel my left leg. It was completely numb. *You're almost done. Keep moving!* I pushed hard at the end and finished strong.

There was no time for a cooldown as the cameras quickly approached, but first I wanted to see my family and friends and give everyone a hug, especially Jill. We clung onto each other. No words needed to be exchanged. Our tears and smiles communicated the unspoken thoughts. The indelible memory in her mind of my comatose and paralyzed body was a sharp contrast to today's milestone of completing an indoor triathlon. I had crossed the threshold of my physical limitations. In my eyes, my body had healed. Thank you, God! That's all there is to say.

CHAPTER TWENTY-THREE

ANSWERING THE QUESTION: AM I HAPPY?

People often ask me what my everyday life is like now that the triathlon is over. They ask about George, and if I ever fell in love again. George is fine. We remain wonderful friends. As for falling in love? The answer is not yet. However, I'm still hopeful that I will be blessed to share my life with a good man.

People also ask if my body is fully healed. The answer is yes and no. Yes, God gave me an amazing gift of recovery. I feel undeserving and praise him every day for this gift. I participated in a triathlon. The message in heaven was, 'Your body will heal,' and my body did – but not completely. I still feel the blatant effects of the accident. Some of the simplest movements of my body require extensive mental and physical effort. My lungs remain compromised, and I often get bronchitis and am at constant risk of pneumonia because I cannot breathe as deeply as I should. I will always suffer from vertigo and therefore never have a true sense of balance. I will need continuous vision therapy as well as my special contact lens and prism glasses to ensure that my eyes will be able to work together and focus. I have a permanent visual disability. I have lost my dream of being a mother. I will never be without weakness on my left side. I will never be capable of holding a full-time job because of the mental and physical exertion required. However, I am amazed by what my body can do, and that's what I focus on. God continues to provide strength and remains faithful.

Because of my injury, I will always be completely dependent on God to help me wake up and live each day. Because I remain weak, his power is made perfect. Because of him, I walk. Because of him, I run. Because of him, I swim. Because of him, I live.

During a newspaper interview, a journalist asked, 'Julie, if you could change anything and take the accident out of your life, would you?'

'No,' I answered with complete sincerity. 'If my accident had not happened, I would not know what I know today, and I would not be who I am today.'

People often ask me, 'Well, did you "go back and be happy?" Are you happy?'

My answer is, 'Yes, but it wasn't easy.' Being happy has been a long-term process and spiritual journey with twelve key stepping-stones along the way: **Faith, Family, Friends, Feelings, Flexibility, Forgiveness, Fearlessness, Fitness, Failure, Fortitude, Finances and Future.**

Perhaps you, too, are facing a difficult journey back from a painful loss such as cancer, divorce, bereavement, addiction, illness, injury, depression or one of the many other debilitating 'thorns' that occur in life. If so, I pray that you might find some of these stepping-stones from my own life to be helpful in your journey to happiness.

Faith: Without faith, I would not be alive today. Faith has become the foundational gravel which paves my path. What an incredible and indelible memory I have from my visit in heaven. After encountering the unconditional love and peace of the Holy Spirit, I understand what a personal relationship with God through Christ means. My faith is no longer blind, but real.

As a child of God, each of us has access to our Heavenly Father. He loves us beyond description. All we have to do is talk to him. Just pray! He wants a personal relationship with each of us. How humbling is that? Many nights, as I lay strapped in the bed at Marianjoy, I called to him. As I ran the triathlon, I called to him. These days on the train, as I commute to my part-time job, I call to him. He is only a prayer away and wants to hear from us.

I will never forget my first time back in church after my accident. While standing in the pew and reciting the Lord's Prayer, I started crying. Speaking the words 'Thy will be done on earth as it is in heaven' made me long once again for that unspeakable peace that I experienced in the light. I knew that my life wouldn't be the same on earth as it was in heaven. Yet throughout my physical recovery and spiritual journey, I learned that faith is a constant act of surrender. The words 'Give us this day our daily bread' truly touch upon the gratitude that overflows within me. I have a thankful heart. God continues to provide my 'daily bread' required for physical sustenance, but more than that, I have experienced first hand the amazing grace of his Son, the Bread of Life. Partaking in that communion is what quenches my spiritual hunger.

Waking up from my coma and discovering that I was completely disabled, I didn't know what my new reality would be. All I clung onto were the words I had heard in heaven, 'Your body will heal.' In a wheelchair at Marianjoy, I surrendered my physical self to God. I accepted the real possibility that I could be in a wheelchair for the rest of my life, and I accepted that. However, I wasn't going to give up on working hard for a full recovery if that was God's will. God is in charge, but we are part of our own healing process, and we need to take an active role. After all, faith is an action.

I want to stress that it wasn't my faith alone, but the prayers of countless others who helped in my recovery. Intercessory prayer is powerful. I will be forever grateful to my friends and the strangers who lifted me and my family in prayer.

Family: Even Dr Shea thinks that the constant outpouring of love and support from my family helped me progress to my fullest possible recovery. They were always there, ready to help me. At Marianjoy, my mother spoon-fed me; Tammy bathed me and Brett recorded music for me to listen to.

My family was and remains my advocate. My dad stopped the hospital staff as I was being wheeled out to be taken to a nursing home. He fought with the insurance company to insist that I instead be taken to a rehabilitation facility. Dad never left my side.

I realize that not everyone has a loving and supportive family, and my heart grieves for those who are facing a struggle on their own. But remember, you have a Heavenly Father who loves you and wants the best for you. He is with you. Always.

Try to connect with someone who can help be your advocate. In the back section, I have compiled a list of agencies and organizations that have resources that can assist.

Something important that I want to address is the change of family dynamics. Be prepared for this shift. It is not an easy one. As part of the ThinkFirst presentations that I make through Central DuPage Hospital, I mention to young drivers that their bad decisions to run a red light or speed around a curve can change an entire family. When one person is injured, the whole family suffers. It's not an isolated incident.

Perhaps you are a family member caring for a loved one who is facing a difficult time. As caregiver, you need to take care of yourself too before you feel overwhelmed. Respite programs are typically available through churches or community organizations that will provide some much needed time away for caregivers. It's like the way we're instructed to breathe from the airplane's oxygen mask first: caregivers must take care of themselves first to be in a better mindset to take care of their loved one.

Friends: Another important lifeline for recovery is friendship. How blessed I feel that my friends supported me through every stage. My closest friends, Sue and Jill, were constantly with me. Consoling me, encouraging me, just being with me. I cannot stress enough the importance of someone who has experienced a life change to still feel that he or she belongs. If one of your friends is suffering through a present hardship, just be there for him or her. Pick up the phone and call. Invite her to dinner. Visit her at the rehabilitation center, hospital or home. Make him feel that he is loved and that you fully accept his physical or mental limitations.

If you are the one facing difficulty, please reach out to your friends. You can usually share with them what you might not be able to discuss with your family. You need to stay connected so you won't disconnect from life. Find new friends through support groups, with people who are going through a similar experience.

During my stay at Marianjoy, I welcomed the opportunity to visit with other patients. We were all different, yet the same. Our lives were completely changed, and because of that, we shared an unspeakable bond. We didn't want to feel different. We all just wanted to belong.

Recently in church, one of the Bible readings was about the story of Jesus healing a paralyzed man. It's about four friends of a paralyzed man. Jesus was visiting their town, and the four men tried to carry their paralyzed friend through a throng of people to reach Jesus, but it was too crowded. However, the friends didn't give up. They cut a hole in the roof above Jesus and, after digging through it, lowered their friend on a mat to place him in front of the one who could restore. Jesus healed this man and said, 'I tell you, get up, take your mat and go home' (Mark 2:11).

When I heard this passage, I wept. The parallels were apparent. I, too, had been told to 'get up, take your mat and go home' when I heard, 'Your body will heal. Go back and be happy.'

But also this passage stressed the importance of friendship. The paralyzed man was blessed. He had persistent friends who were there for him, supporting him and literally carrying him to someone they knew who could help him. I am grateful that my friends never gave up on me and continue to be there for me.

Feelings: It doesn't matter what you are going through right now, please communicate and express your feelings. Don't keep them bottled in. Don't lock others out of your life. If you are in that dark place right now, please reach out for help. Please speak with someone about how you are feeling. I know what it feels like to be trapped. It's the loneliest place to be. However, don't remain isolated. Reach out. For me, I reached out to Sister Val. I needed answers. I needed direction. I felt lost. Up until a year ago, I occasionally saw a psychologist who specialized in brain injury. Now, fifteen years after my accident, I only continue to speak with Sister Val for spiritual guidance. Professionals are able to provide strategic perspective and validate the feelings. Recently, I met with two teens, Katie and Frank. They are both traumatic brain injury survivors who have made great strides in their physical recovery. Katie was in a terrible car accident, and Frank was injured while skiing. I encouraged both of them to speak about their feelings. It's important to focus on the physical and the emotional impact of an injury.

The first question anyone seems to ask after a life-changing event is 'Why?' In my situation, the answer was because a teenage boy ran a red light. The accident was avoidable. For a long time, I was stuck at 'Why?' But after surrendering my condition to God and accepting the present reality, I was then able to move on with my life. When life shatters like Humpty Dumpty, however, you need to get help with putting the pieces back in the right place. I know how hard it is to reach out for help. It's the epitome of vulnerability. But ultimately, you need to accept what has happened. Recently, a dear friend underwent a double mastectomy after being diagnosed with breast cancer during a routine mammogram. Since she lives in another state I wasn't able to visit her, but we spoke on the phone often while she recovered. Even though a severe brain stem injury and breast cancer are completely different, we shared a common experience: a life-changing event which was both physical and psychological. My being able to relate to her feelings helped. She didn't feel alone or isolated. She didn't have to explain her feelings of vulnerability, disappointment, frustration, and anger. I just knew. We both understood the feeling of being an open wound.

Flexibility: I will always remember Dr Shea's advice when I felt so overwhelmed. 'Julie,' he said, 'your accident was not only a physical event, it was a psychological one. Yes, it was and continues to be an emotional event.'

That's a huge stepping-stone: accepting and learning to be comfortable in the body that you now have. Like an identity thief, this injury stole away the life I knew and lived. That is the crime of a traumatic brain injury. It often steals memories from your past and takes away your identity in the present as well as your former dreams for the future. It is up to each individual to reclaim what it is that he or she feels was stolen as a result of injury or illness. Acceptance of the new reality is a major step in this process. Flexibility is one of the best defenses against adversity. Accepting and adapting enable one to move forward along the gravel path. It's not the yellow brick road, but it's a path that leads to a future.

Forgiveness: The act of forgiveness heals you. Letting go of the anger, the despair and the hurt released the energy that I was directing toward fueling those feelings. Forgiving is not an easy thing to do, but it's an act of grace.

Dialing the phone to speak with the teenager who ran into my car was difficult. I had harbored feelings of bitterness against him. His irresponsible decision to speed through a red light wrecked my life. His actions took away my physical ability to hold down a full-time job. I could no longer count on my body to work the way it used to. However, I realized that for my healing to progress, I had to speak with him. I needed to hear myself forgive him. I heard the despair in his voice as he apologized for what he had caused. I felt compassion. With the deepest sincerity, I told him, 'I forgive you. It's time for you to forgive yourself.'

By letting go of my anger and hurt, I was able to untangle myself from destructive emotions. By forgiving, I was no longer a victim. Perhaps you need to forgive someone in your life. Perhaps you need to forgive yourself. Let go of the past so you can move forward to your future.

172

As the Dutch physician and botanist Paul Boese once said, 'Forgiveness does not change the past, but it does enlarge the future.'

Fearlessness: Not being afraid was another key stepping-stone. Waking up to a disabled body is frightening. My fear of the unknown was tangible. What had happened to me? What was going to happen to me? However, I clung to my memory of the peace I felt in the light. I wasn't afraid of dying, but I was afraid of living in a severely disabled body.

To move forward, I had to confront my fears and of course surrender them to God. He was and is in control. I tried to start setting goals for myself. By narrowing the scope of daily tasks I could complete, I worked hard to check them off my list. As I recovered, my list of goals grew longer in content and in time frame. In Marianjoy, I remember starting that list as I touched each broken part of my body in disbelief. When I touched my stomach, which was attached to a tube, I thought 'Okay, that doesn't work. What am I going to do about this?' Then I touched my left arm, which lay limp across my chest, and said, 'Okay, that doesn't work. What am I going to do about this?' I continued to confront everything about my body that wasn't working.

Fear has been an everyday side effect of my accident. I no longer feel physically safe in a car as a passenger or as a driver. Confronting this fear was huge for me. In order to regain independence and have a way to get to work, I had to get back behind the wheel. Yet even today, I drive my car with an undeniable fear of an accident which would once again send me back to a rehabilitation facility. I never want to feel trapped again.

My fear of the water was another hurdle to face. Taking that first breath to go beneath the water's surface was like facing a dragon with fire spewing from its mouth. Frightening. Yet, I knew that it was something that needed to be done for my recovery.

Faith is action, and action can conquer fear. Instead of lying in bed at Marianjoy and allowing myself to be swallowed by the overwhelming circumstances of my life-changing event, I chose to press the faith button. I prayed. Prayer is the best defense against fear. Surrendering my condition to God, I knew that ultimately, his will would determine the outcome. But meanwhile, I was ready to work hard to achieve whatever recovery was possible.

Take a quiet moment and pray. Surrender your situation to God. Press the faith button. And be prepared to take action on the paths that the Lord sets before you.

Fitness: Even when I was severely disabled, fitness was important to me. It was always an integral part of my life, and I had promised God that I would work hard for my physical recovery after my accident. Fitness took a different form when I woke up disabled. I depended on others to move my body, which was important in order to prevent the continuation of atrophy.

Many rehabilitation programs offer pool exercises as well as other physical therapies. As I participated in outpatient rehabilitation therapy, I let my therapist know what my physical goals were. I was my own advocate and let her know that I wanted to try to walk again. At that point, I could only walk ten feet on my own without a wheelchair. Although my desire seemed improbable to the therapist, she still listened and worked with me on that specific goal.

Even though there was a likelihood that I would have remained in the wheelchair, I still envisioned a fitness program for myself which included core balance strengthening and weight training for my upper body. Under the direction of a medical professional, these options can be realistic even to someone confined to a wheelchair. It's important for a person who feels physically trapped in his or her own body to have an outlet. Finding a form of fitness that works for him or her will be rewarding. In addition, I continue to work hard on my vision fitness through vision therapy sessions with Dr. Margolis.

Failure: You need to be willing to fail in order to succeed. Repeatedly, I fell when I tried to stand, but I kept trying. When I had learned to stand, I fell when I tried to walk, but I kept trying. Although nothing was fair about what happened to me, I had two choices: wallow or walk. I chose to try to walk. Commit to memory an empowering verse: Philippians 4:13 – 'I can do all things through Christ who gives me strength.'

The most hurtful failure, however, was getting fired because of my disability. Never in my life would I expect to experience firsthand discrimination against the disabled. Previously, I had always exceeded the standards of an employer's expectations. My job reviews were always outstanding until the accident. Although my Lithuanian work ethic remained intact, my ability to work had been taken away, along with the financial security which my work ethic guaranteed.

Through each failure, I tried to learn something that would help me to do better in my next attempt. It's okay to fail. And after being unfairly fired because of my disability, I found the strength to stand up against something that was wrong. I took my former employer to court for discrimination under the Americans with Disabilities Act.

And remember, just because you might fail at something does not mean you are a failure. It just means you tried something, and it didn't work.

Fortitude: Dr Shea once said to me, 'Julie, even though you're severely disabled, you always knew that you could still make a contribution. You not only made a contribution, but also a commitment to live and find your purpose.' Grinning, he continued, 'Do you know what the difference is between a contribution and a commitment? The answer is at the breakfast table. The hen contributed the eggs, but the pig who provided the bacon made the real commitment.' Through his illustration, Dr Shea provided real insight into fortitude. He was right. It was that inner strength and determination which drove me to the finish line. I couldn't give up. Just as my mom always told me, 'This is our place of work. We get our gift of rest when we get to heaven.' It's not easy, but God will give you the strength as you find and connect with your own inner strength. During an interview session, Margaret asked Dr Shea what his advice would be for other brain injury survivors and their families. Without a pause, he stated, 'Never give up hope.'

Finances: Financial security is a tough subject, especially for me. The loss of my physical security and ability to work affected my financial security. Although I am grateful that the United States has such programs in place for people with disabilities, it is humbling for me to depend on a government-sponsored disability program to meet my daily needs. As a child who was taught to be self-sufficient and work hard in life to earn a good living, I am frustrated at not being able to work the way in which I desired. However, I count my blessings that I hold a part-time job with the law firm of Romanucci and Blandin and can partially pay for my living expenses through their employment.

No matter what amount you may have, it's important to establish a financial plan that works. I have learned how to be a creative value shopper. Recently, I was complimented on my winter jacket. The person had no idea that it was three years old and had cost me only $18 at Wal-Mart.

I strongly recommend that you or an advocate obtain trustworthy financial advice. You need to plan long-term. The most important lesson I have learned is to ask for help. There are family members and friends who will most likely help if they can.

Future: The stepping-stones of my faith, family, friends, forgiveness, feelings, flexibility, fearlessness, fitness, failure, fortitude, and finances all prepared me for my future. Although my future became a totally different reality than I had ever imagined, I still had a future.

Last year, my psychologist advised me that she felt that I had benefited as much as I could from therapy sessions. I didn't need to go back and see her anymore. I had emotionally healed. During our last session, she asked me what it was that helped me the most, beyond what I had already shared about my stepping-stones. Taking a moment to reflect, I said aloud what it was – finding a future. From the senselessness of my accident and injuries, I found a purpose – to share my story.

Recently, I heard a Chinese proverb. 'If you want to find happiness for an hour, take a nap. If you want to find happiness for a day, go fishing. If you want to find happiness for the rest of your life, help others.' That quest would become my future. Helping others would become my fulfillment.

During one of my darkest moments, Dr Shea asked me to meet with families of brain injury survivors. His wisdom of providing a purpose ultimately saved my life. That is the void in everyone's life that needs to be filled and validated. We all need a purpose. We all want to help and feel needed.

Writing this book has been a major fulfillment. I am grateful that Monarch provided this opportunity to me so I could share my story with you. At first, I felt the injury defined who I was: a traumatic brain injury statistic. During the healing process, however, I discovered that I am not my injury. The injury is something that happened to me, but it is not who I am. Perhaps you might feel the same way right now, too. Maybe you feel that your condition defines who you are. Don't allow your situation to steal your identity. It's just something that happened to you, it's not who you are. Stop the identity thief and put your life in proper perspective.

You have a future. Perhaps it's nothing like the one you had in mind, but it is still your future. One of my favorite verses is Jeremiah 29:11, which reads, "'For I know the plans I have for you," declares the Lord, "plans to prosper you and not to harm you, plans to give you hope and a future.'"

Isn't that powerful? God has plans, hope and a future for each of us. I hold tight to that promise every day. We don't have control over how long our future will be, but every single day is a gift, waiting to be unwrapped and enjoyed.

So how do you find your future? Pray. Speak to God like he is really listening because he is. Reach out to friends and family who can help support you along the way. Acknowledge your feelings and accept your circumstances and condition. Forgive the people who have really disappointed you before, during and after what happened. Forgive yourself. Face your greatest fears. Be prepared to fail in order to move forward to your future. Be flexible, because we don't always know what happens in life. Find the fortitude to believe in yourself, to believe that you can go beyond your disabling injury or illness. Make a financial plan to help provide for your future.

So, to answer the question, Am I happy? Yes. Trust me, I'm not living a 'happily ever after' scenario, but who is? I have inner joy. It has been a long journey, but I arrived at a place where I can punctuate my joy with an exclamation point.

One of my favorite verses is now Psalm 118:24: *'This is the day the Lord has made; let us rejoice and be glad in it.'* Each morning I recite this verse, grateful that the Lord allowed me to wake up to another day and grateful that I can share his story of hope and joy.

Pastor Jane Kunzie-Brunner, a minister at Lutheran Church of the Atonement in Barrington, Illinois, said: 'Joy is a choice, a discipline, and a gift.' I chose to go back and be happy!

Resources

Please note that these resources are obtained from publicly available resources. If you discover any inaccuracy in the phone numbers listed, please call information at 1-800-555-1212 for toll-free listings or 411 for local service.

Brain Injury Clubhouse

A not-for-profit organization designed for adults who have sustained any type of brain injury. The Clubhouse aims to improve the overall quality of life for both members and their families. Located nationally, Clubhouses are operated by and for the members, all of whom are survivors of a brain injury. Members rely on each other for support socially, emotionally, and developmentally and are recognized for their abilities, not their disabilities.

Midwest Brain Injury Clubhouse
1010 North Hooker Street, Suite 302
Chicago, Illinois 60622
(312) 932-1120
www.braininjuryclubhouse.org

Cornerstone Clubhouse
781 Richmond Street
London, Ontario N6A 3H4
(519) 679-6809
www.cornerstoneclubhouse.com

High Desert Roads
1129 Girard NE
Albuquerque, New Mexico 87106

High Street Clubhouse
1101 East High Street, Suite B
Charlottesville, Virginia 22902
www.vanc.org

Hy Feinstein Clubhouse
65 Austin Blvd.
Commack, New York 11725
(631) 543-2245
www.lihia.org/feinstein.htm

MossRehab Clubhouse
7612 Dungan Road
Philadelphia, Pennsylvania 19111
(215) 745-9766

MossRehab Clubhouse
135 South Broad Street
Woodbury, New Jersey 08096
(856) 853-9900, ext. 101

Opportunity Place
90 Millburn Avenue, 2nd Floor
Milburn, New Jersey 07041
(973) 275-5200

Side by Side Clubhouse
1001 Main Street
Stone Mountain, Georgia 30083
(404) 378-1139
www.sidebysideclubhouse.org

Hanson House
173 Front Street
Berea, Ohio 44017
1-440-234-9900
www.hansonbiclubhouse.org

Integrity House
2043 N. Broadway
Santa Ana, California 92706
1-714-542-0855
www.integrity-house.org

Opportunity Project
60 E. Willow Street
Millburn, New Jersey 07041
1-973-921-1000
www.opportunityproject.org

Adapt Clubhouse
8136 Keene Mill Road
Suite B102
Springfield, Virginia 22152
1-703-451-8881
www.braininjrusvcs.org

Ballinger Clubhouse
P.O. Box 26453
Akron, Ohio 44319
1-330-724-4000
www.ballingerclubhouse.org

Denbigh House
12725 McManus Boulevard
Suite 2E
Newport News, Virginia 23602
1-757-833-7845
www.communityfuturesva.org

International Brain Injury Association

P.O. Box 1804
Alexandria, Virginia 22313
1-703-960-6500
www.internationalbrain.org

The International Brain Injury Association (IBIA) is dedicated to the development and support of multidisciplinary medical and clinical professionals, advocates, policy makers, consumers and others who work to improve outcomes and opportunities for persons with brain injury.

Brain Injury Association of America (BIAA)

1608 Spring Hill Road
Suite 110
Vienna, Virginia 22182
1-703-761-0750.
Toll-free helpline (800) 444-6443
www.biausa.org

The mission of BIAA is to create a better future through brain injury prevention, research, education, and advocacy. BIAA and its affiliates reach millions of individuals living with the 'silent epidemic' of brain injury by acting as a clearinghouse of community service information and resources, participating in legislative advocacy, facilitating prevention awareness, hosting education programs, and encouraging research.

The BIAA website has helpful links to other resources such as Head Injury Hotline, Concussion Safety, SABER (Strategic Alliance for Brain Injury Enhanced Recovery), Recovery Awareness Foundation, NASHIA (National Association of State Head Injury Administrators), CDC (Centers for Disease Control and Prevention) and their SafeUSA section, IARP (International Association of Rehabilitation Professionals), The Brain Injury Society, TBI Model Systems Project, and the ThinkFirst Foundation.

The following chart shows data compiled and arranged by the BIAA.

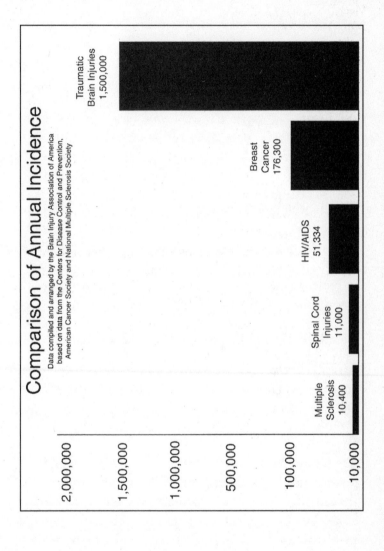

Comparison of Annual Incidence

Data compiled and arranged by the Brain Injury Association of America based on data from the Centers for Disease Control and Prevention, American Cancer Society and National Multiple Sclerosis Society

Traumatic Brain Injuries 1,500,000

Breast Cancer 176,300

HIV/AIDS 51,334

Spinal Cord Injuries 11,000

Multiple Sclerosis 10,400

2,000,000
1,500,000
1,000,000
500,000
100,000
10,000

Brain Injury Association of South Africa

P.O. Box 2368
Pinetown
KwaZulu-Natal
3650
031-767-0348152

The Rehabilitation Institute of Chicago

345 E. Superior Street
Chicago, Illinois 60611
1-312-238-1000
1-866-999-3344
www.ric.org

The Rehabilitation Institute of Chicago (RIC) has been recognized as "the #1 Rehabilitation Hospital in America" since 1991 by U.S. News & World Report. Founded in 1954, RIC has earned a worldwide reputation as being a leader in patient care, advocacy, research and educating health professionals in physical medicine and rehabilitation.

Rehabilitation Institute of Chicago Life Center

345 East Superior Street
Chicago, Illinois 60611
(800) 354-REHAB
(312) 238-1000
www.ric.org

Life Center embraces the themes of 'L' for learning, 'I' for innovation, 'F' for family, and 'E' for empowerment. It is the center's hope that access to the various resources found in the Life Center will assist persons with disabilities and their families in developing their capabilities to their fullest potential.

Rehabilitation Institute of Chicago Women with Disabilities Center

345 East Superior Street, Room 164
Chicago, Illinois 60611
(312) 238-1051

The Center is dedicated to providing services that empower women and girls with disabilities to practice self-determination in achieving emotional and physical wellness. To meet this goal, the Center provides services free of charge centered on advocacy, support, education, and combating the inherent isolation of women and teenage girls with disabilities.

National Spinal Cord Injury Association (NSCIA)

National Office: (800) 962-9629
Resource Center: (301) 588-6959
www.spinalcord.org

The mission of the NSCIA is to educate and empower survivors of spinal cord injury and disease through the toll-free help line, nationwide chapters, and support groups to achieve and maintain higher levels of independence.

Spinal Injuries Association England

SIA House
2 Trueman Place
Oldbrook
Milton Keynes
MK6 2HH
0845 678 6633
freephone advice line 0800 980 0501
sia@spinal.uk

Spinal Cord Injury Association Australia

1 Jennifer Street
Little Bay NSW 2036
02-9661-8855
800-819-775 (for people outside of Sydney)
office@scia.org.au

ThinkFirst

29W120 Butterfield Road
Suite 105
Warrenville, Illinois 60555
(800) THINK-56
1-630-393-1400
www.thinkfirst.org

Leading injury prevention through education, research and policy.

Access Living

115 West Chicago Avenue
Chicago, Illinois 60610
(312) 640-2100
Toll-free helpline 1-800-613-8549
generalinfo@accessliving.org
www.accessliving.org

Access Living advocates on behalf of and provides services to people with disabilities. It fosters the dignity, pride and self-esteem of people with disabilities and enhances the options available to them so they may choose and maintain individualized and satisfying lifestyles.

Save a Life Foundation (SALF)

9950 W. Lawrence Avenue
Suite 300
Schiller Park, Illinois 60176
(847) 928-9683
www.salf.org

The mission of SALF is to heighten public awareness, to promote and train basic life-supporting first aid skills.

National Suicide Prevention Lifeline

Hotline: (800) 273-TALK
For deaf and hard of hearing TTY: (800) 799-TTY
(1-800-799-4889)
www.suicidepreventionlifeline.org

Vision Therapy Resources:

College of Optometrists in Vision Development

215 West Garfield Road
Suite 210
Aurora, Ohio 44202
(888) 268-3770
www.covd.org

This college was formed for the primary purposes of establishing a body of practitioners who are knowledgeable in functional and developmental concepts of vision and who will ensure that the public will receive continually improving vision care.

Parents Active for Vision Education (PAVE)

4135 54th Place
San Diego, California 92105-2303
(800) PAVE-988
www.pavevision.org

A non-profit resource and support organization whose mission is to raise public awareness of the crucial relationship between vision and achievement.

Neuro-Optometric Rehabilitation Association (NORA)

(866) 222-3887

www.nora.cc

NORA is an eclectic of professionals focused to advance the art and science of rehabilitation/habilitation of the neurologically and cognitively injured and disabled survivor population and their families.